Quiet Paris

Siobhan Wall

Quiet Paris

Siobhan Wall

F

FRANCES LINCOLN LIMITED

PUBLISHERS

Frances Lincoln Limited
www.franceslincoln.com

Quiet Paris
Copyright © Frances Lincoln Limited 2013
Text and photographs copyright © Siobhan Wall 2013
Artworks copyright ©: p.122–3 Gael Davrinche;
p. 124 Raphaël Zarka; p.125 right Mehdi-Georges Lahlou;
p.127 Éric Dessert from the exhibition 'Une Autre Chine';
p.128 Bernard Moninot;
p.129 Diego Romero from the exhibition 'A Free Spirit Potter';
p.132 Manon de Pauw; p.133 Peter Callesen

First Frances Lincoln edition 2013

A catalogue record for this book is available from the British Library.

ISBN: 978-0-7112-3343-0

Printed and bound in China

9

COVER Le Repaire de Cartouche; BACK COVER Restaurant de La Maison
de l'Amerique Latine; PAGE 1 Les Jardins des Archives Nationales;
PAGES 2–3 Le Jardin du Musée Rodin; OPPOSITE Place Vendôme;
PAGES 6–7 Hôtel du Jeu de Paume garden; PAGE 8 view from
Square Louise Michel, Montmartre

Contents

Introduction

Paris is one of the world's most beautiful cities, with astounding architecture, richly endowed museums, chic boutiques, small patisseries and stylish restaurants, and host to a huge variety of gastronomic and visual delights. The city is not only fascinating but also quite compact so it's possible to visit the medieval Museé de Cluny in the morning, ascend the imposing Montparnasse Tower for a panoramic view over lunch and then take an afternoon walk round the ambitious La Grande Arche de la Défense. Because the city has so much to offer, certain areas become very crowded and for Parisians the demands of urban life can sometimes become overwhelming. There is a different, calmer side to the city, however, best appreciated in a slower way, on foot. In the 1960s the Situationist philosopher Guy Debord wrote eloquently about the pleasures of wandering aimlessly through the city as an inventive way to resist the over-commercialisation of public spaces. Today, there are so many visually intrusive posters demanding that we buy the latest electronic gadget and it is getting harder to avoid the ubiquitous brand name stores replicated all over the world. Buying clothes or household objects tends to be a familiar and often boring experience, denying curious shoppers any possibility of a serendipitous encounter with the maker of a pair of gorgeous suede shoes or an individually thrown porcelain vase. There are alternatives to being lost and confused in a huge, soulless department store, however. Eschewing the factory-made and the predictable, many of the people working in the independent shops featured in the pages of *Quiet Paris* have either made the items on sale themselves or buy from French designers who devote as much attention to creating a glazed jug as a wine grower will to their best vintage.

With so many guidebooks written about the fascinations of Paris, it might seem impossible to discover anywhere new that hasn't already been visited en masse. Walking around, I wondered whether we are now less familiar with losing our way and coming across places by benign accident rather than pre-ordained design, especially with the emergence of roaming technology. There are ways to slip under the net of the tourist map, however, even in such an abundantly photographed metropolis. It didn't take long for me to discover a small antiquarian bookshop in rue Condorcet that didn't have a telephone or even a website, for instance. This could only happen whilst walking expectantly though the city, as an internet search for this shop would have been futile.

One thing that soon became apparent while seeking out intriguing quiet places was that independent bookshops are still thriving in France. Booksellers love talking about books, whether this means introducing readers to the soft, tactile qualities of a diary handmade from fragments of old postcards or a sophisticated photobook about radical designs in contemporary architecture. There are fewer quiet boutiques in the city. It was a delight to discover a small gift and homeware shop in the 11th arrondissement one afternoon, but after complimenting the young woman on her unusual items and the fact her shop didn't play music, she became very apologetic. She said that she had only been open a week so the hi-fi hadn't yet arrived, and that the lively atmosphere she had hoped for was missing. It was hard to convince her that the quietness was rather attractive – and different to other places. So it was a real pleasure finding rare, muzac-free shops, bistros or cafés. More often than not, in boutiques on streets such as rue Charlot, the welcoming owner is also the designer and seamstress of the exquisite clothes hanging in the window. There seems to be nowhere else where expertise is valued so highly as in Paris, the city where innovation and the desire for novelty is perfectly married with a profound respect for skills passed down by masters of a patiently-acquired craft.

One less inspiring aspect of Paris that locals are all too familiar with, however, is the fact that property is very expensive so apartments tend to be tiny, often consisting of a single room with a kitchenette and shower room at one end. Gardens are rare and most balconies consist of no more than a box of a few red geraniums carefully balanced on a windowsill. What this means is that public spaces tend to be crowded as Parisians avoid indoor claustrophobia by walking round and round local gardens with their small dogs and children. Every inch of green space is used, so you might see a group of Chinese women practising Tai Chi on the small Square de Temple lawn whilst their husbands play table tennis the other side of the path.

So where are the ideal places to escape the hustle and bustle of this lovely city? The Périphérique acts as a man-made border surrounding the central arrondisements so only serene places inside this clearly demarcated boundary have been included. The larger public gardens such as the Jardin du Palais Royal and the Jardin des Plants have nice vistas, but are too well known and don't feel secret or secluded. It soon became apparent that the periphery of parks and gardens are often the quietest spots. The shady, tree-lined terrace inbetween the elegant Jeu de Paume photography museum and the wide expanse of Les Tuileries is a perfect spot to sit and read a book, for example. On sunny afternoons warm breezes carry the scent of lavender from nearby herbaceous borders and it is easy to feel at a remove from the sight of strolling families far below.

The hilly Square Louise Michel on the edge of Montmartre also has some remarkably tranquil places to sit, and yet, just two minutes walk away there are ant-like streams of visitors steadily climbing the steps to the Basilica Sacre Coeur, totally unaware of the large-leaved exotic plants growing nearby. In the west, the modern, walled gardens tucked behind the main path in the Parc André Citroën are surprisingly rural yet this is only one train stop further on from the Eiffel Tower. The modern parks are also very accessible and the organisation www.bleucommeuneorange.com organise tours of Paris for disabled people.

Just wandering a bit off the beaten track can offer a glimpse of another, quieter side to Paris, and as the city is very built up, tranquil corners feel really precious. It is also worth appreciating the less obvious places to wander, such as the smaller streets off the main roads where local delicatessens, small hammams or artists' studios appear just when you least expect them.

An artist in Belleville told me that Parisians devour culture like food, but instead of queuing up for hours with everyone else who is longing to see the latest irresistible show, a visit to an independent gallery can reveal new talent or intriguing work rarely seen elsewhere. Avoiding the crowded 'vernissage' or exhibition opening means you will be more likely to be able to appreciate the artworks on display. As in every large city, a refusal to follow the crowds can lead the curious in interesting, unpredictable, and often quite fortuitous directions, and this book quietly encourages readers to discover intriguing places hidden behind the imperial facades of Haussman's grand boulevards. Go in search of the Tea Caddy near to Notre Dame Cathedral for afternoon tea or have an early supper at restaurant Polidor near La Sorbonne on the Left Bank, both of which, along with a few other long established places to eat and drink, still remain music-free. And when you have walked far enough for one day and want to find a peaceful room in an apartment or hotel, *Quiet Paris* will tell you the perfect place to enjoy thoughtful conversation about the gardens you have seen, the books you have read and the food you have tasted in this entrancing city.

Museums

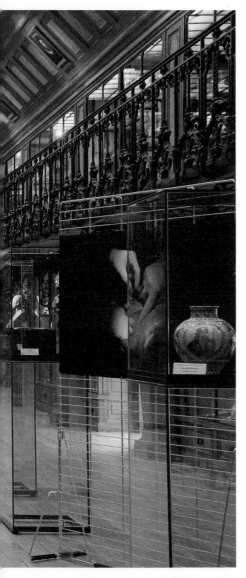

Musée d'Histoire de la Médecine

12 rue de l'Ecole de Médecine, 75006 ☎ 01 76 53 16 93
€ parisdescartes.fr/eng/culture/
Open 1 September–15 July, daily 2pm–5.30pm, closed Thursday, Sunday and public holidays. From 15 July–31 August, open daily 2pm–5.30pm, closed Saturday, Sunday and 15 August. Closed between Christmas and New Year
Métro Odéon **Bus** 21, 27, 38, 58, 63, 85, 86, 87
There is a lift to the main floor of the museum but the stairs to the balcony make this upper area inaccessible

Situated inside the Paris Descartes University Medical School, this small museum of the history of medicine is a testament to the remarkable advances made through scientific endeavour in the past 500 years. The collection is one of the oldest in Europe and includes not only an array of antique medical instruments but also a rather gruesome teaching aid – a model of a flayed male body. More appealing, perhaps, are the anatomical models, including a mannequin from the late 18th century made entirely of wood which can be taken apart to reveal the interior organs. In one corner you can even see the portable dissection kit used to examine Napoleon after his death on the island of Elba. Intriguing temporary exhibitions are held in the main room and complement the antique instruments on permanent display.

Musée des Arts et Métiers

60 rue Réaumur, 75003 ☎ 01 53 01 82 00 **€** but free the first Sunday of the month and Thursday after 6pm
www.arts-et-metiers.net **Open** Tuesday–Sunday 10am–6pm, Thursday to 9.30pm, closed Monday, 25 December, 1 May
Métro Arts et Métiers, Réaumur-Sébastopol **Bus** 20, 38, 39, 47
The museum has excellent disabled access and wheelchairs are available for loan with a current, valid ID or passport.
There are also special events for people with a visual impairment as well as adults and children with learning difficulties

The name of this museum translates as 'Arts and Crafts' but in fact it houses an extraordinary collection of scientific instruments, machines and inventions. One of the most spectacular rooms can be found in the former Abbey of Saint Martin Des Champs with its stunning display of aeronautical endeavour. Hanging high above a curved viewing ramp is the Blériot XI, the plane used in 1909 to fly across the English Channel for the first time. Nearby is Foucault's pendulum, which appeared in the novel by Umberto Eco, and at the top of nearby stairs Clement Adler's 1897 mesmerising bat-like monoplane. The entire museum is full of astonishing machines, from 19th-century toy automata to a display of old penny farthing bicycles (velocipèdes) and even an early supercomputer.

Musée Zadkine

100 bis rue d'Assas, 75006 ☎ 01 55 42 77 20
Free for permanent display € for temporary exhibitions
www.zadkine.paris.fr **Open** daily 10am–6pm, closed Monday and public holidays
Métro Notre-Dame des Champs, Vavin **RER** Port-Royal **Bus** 38, 82, 83, 91
The building is mostly wheelchair accessible except for the toilet facilities (the website has a map specifying which rooms are accessible)

A Russian artist who emigrated to Paris in the 1920s, Ossip Zadkine (1908–67) produced over 400 sculptures, many of which can be seen in this small museum dedicated to his life and work. It is a delightful space to visit, from walking through the cottage garden to discovering the gentle, hand-carved figures on large plinths in each tranquil room. This is the perfect atelier for an artist and it is no wonder Zadkine chose to live and work here from 1928 until his death. His semi-abstract ebony and red wood sculptures are unexpectedly quiet to look at and as Zadkine's work introduces us to an important chapter in modernist aesthetics, it is surprising that it is not better recognised.

Musée Cernuschi / Musée des Arts de l'Asie de la Ville de Paris
7 avenue Vélasquez, 75008 ☎ 01 53 96 21 50
Free for permanent collection **€** for temporary exhibitions
www.cernuschi.paris.fr **Open** Tuesday–Sunday 10am–6pm, closed Monday and public holidays
Métro Monceau, Villiers **Bus** 30, 84, 90
The museum has excellent disabled access to all floors

In 1896, the wealthy financier Henry Cernuschi left his grand mansion and his extensive collection of Far Eastern art to the City of Paris. As a result, the Museum of Asian Arts of the City of Paris was created, housing some fascinating artefacts, including a stunning collection of ancient Chinese art, rare Neolithic pottery and an impressive collection of Chinese paintings from the last century. In contrast to the huge, black stone effigy of Buddha, the prehistoric tomb offerings nearby seem surprisingly humble, especially the small terracotta piglets in a pigsty. This is a good opportunity to see how a wealthy Parisian spent the equivalent of his 'gap year' collecting precious objects during an extended world tour. The temporary exhibitions are also fascinating, and have included a survey of work by Chinese artists currently living in Paris.

Musée Guimet
(Musée national des arts asiatiques Guimet)

6 place d'Iéna, 75016 ☎ 01 56 52 53 00
€ www.guimet.fr
Open Wednesday–Monday 10am–6pm, closed Tuesday, 1 January, 1 May, 25 December
Métro Iéna, Boissière **Bus** 22, 30, 32, 63, 82
The museum has excellent access for people with a disability, except for the annex, Les Galeries du Panthéon Bouddhique (Buddhist sculpture galleries), at 19 avenue d'Iéna which are not accessible

The spacious National Museum of Asian Arts is a real pleasure to wander round. This well-lit, air-conditioned museum contains an incredibly diverse range of religious artefacts and everyday objects. Discover ceramics from Korea, Sanskrit bronzes from India or ancient Tibetan masks and exquisite woven textiles. In addition to the permanent exhibits of ancient stone sculptures and precious relics from over 17 Asian countries, temporary exhibitions on contemporary calligraphy, photography and other Asian arts are held here. When you are in need of refreshment, the café in the basement serves a limited range of Southeast Asian dishes but fortunately doesn't play piped music. The museum also has a beautiful 19th-century annex; Les Galeries du Panthéon Bouddhique, which has a tranquil Japanese garden with bamboo trees and a small pond. This doesn't seem to be open during official opening hours, however, so ring in advance to enquire about access.

Musée Nissim de Camondo

63 rue de Monceau, 75008 ☎ 01 53 89 06 50 / 40
€ www.lesartsdecoratifs.fr
Open Wednesday–Sunday 10am–5.30pm, closed Monday and Tuesday
Métro Villiers, Monceau **Bus** 30, 84, 94
The ground floor is accessible but there is no lift for the upper floors

Although this monumental villa was only built in 1911, this museum houses an outstanding collection of French furniture and paintings from the 18th and 19th centuries. Moïse de Camondo was a wealthy banker who intended to bequeath his exquisite objets d'art to his son Nissim. Sadly the young man was killed during the First World War so Moïse donated the building and its contents to the Musée des Arts Decoratifs who now manage this grand house near to Parc Monceau. Walking round this opulent mansion is one of the highlights of a visit to the capital. From the shiny copper pans in the huge kitchen to the satin covered chairs and inlaid walnut tables in the drawing rooms, this is an exceptional place to see period furniture and fittings in a magnificent setting.

Musée Bourdelle

18 rue Antoine Bourdelle, 75015 ☎ 01 49 54 73 73
€ www.bourdelle.paris.fr
Open Tuesday–Sunday 10am–6pm, closed Monday and public holidays
Métro Montparnasse–Bienvenüe, Falguière **Bus** 28, 48, 58, 88, 89, 91, 92, 94, 95, 96
The building is partially accessible for wheelchair users, with accessible toilets on the ground floor near the entrance

Walking down the street, the first thing you notice when approaching this large museum is a giant bronze horse in a garden full of imposing, heroic sculptures. The incredibly prolific 19th-century artist Antoine Bourdelle (1861–1929) lived and worked in these grand buildings. To accommodate his extensive bronze and marble oeuvre, his former studio has recently been enlarged and it seems as if the interior is an ever-expanding space. From the light-filled grand hall with Greek inspired monumental statues to the smaller nymphs and female busts in the rear atelier, this capacious museum is a fascinating insight into the life and works of a truly impressive Parisian.

Jeu de Paume
(Centre Nationale de Photographie)
1 place de la Concorde, 75008
☎ 01 47 03 12 50
€ www.jeudepaume.org
Open Tuesday 11pm–9pm, Wednesday–Sunday 11pm–7pm, closed Monday and most public holidays
Métro Concorde **Bus** 24, 42, 72, 73, 84, 94
The entire building is wheelchair accessible

This elegant building next to Les Tuileries gardens was constructed by Napoléon III and has been used as an exhibition space since the early 20th century. One of the foremost non-profit institutions showing photography in France, this is the ideal location to see temporary exhibitions of work from the advent of the medium to the 21st century. The building was renovated in 1987 and with its white marble staircase and simple design, the interior architecture creates a peaceful ambience for viewing the exhibitions. The small café on the first floor doesn't play music but, unfortunately, the refrigerated cabinets hum rather loudly. On the ground floor a small but well-stocked bookshop stocks an extensive collection of monographs and books focusing on philosophical debates around photographic practice.

Tour Jean Sans Peur

20 rue Étienne Marcel, 75002
☎ 01 40 26 20 28
€ www.tourjeansanspeur.com
Open In summer Wednesday–Sunday
1.30pm–6pm, closed on public holidays.
In winter Wednesday, Saturday and
Sunday 1.30pm–6pm, closed over the
Christmas period
Métro Étienne Marcel, Les Halles
RER Chatelet les Halles **Bus** 29, 38, 47
The tower is not accessible for wheelchair
users

The Tower of John Without Fear was
built between 1409 and 1411, but looks
surprisingly solid considering its age.
The look of the museum could be described
as 'medieval minimalism', as each floor is
sparsely furnished and there are very few
objects on show. Instead, fabric panels tell
illustrated histories about the fearless John
and his tower and there are some beautiful
stone carvings of oak leaves on the ceiling
of the ancient spiral staircase. Temporary
exhibitions on medieval food, animals,
viticulture and other themes are also shown
in the basement.

Musée d'Art et d'Histoire du Judaïsme

Hôtel de Saint-Aignan, 71 rue du Temple, 75003 ☎ 01 53 01 86 60
€ www.mahj.org
Open Sunday–Friday 11am–6pm, Wednesday until 9pm, closed on Saturday, 1 May, 1 January, Yom Kippur and Hoch
Hachanah but open Christmas and Easter
Métro Rambuteau, Hôtel de Ville **RER** Châtelet-Les Halles **Bus** 29, 38, 47, 75
There is good disabled access to the exhibition spaces but not to the library and videothèque

The Museum of Jewish History was opened in the late 1980s and tells the story of Jewish communities in Paris from the
Middle Ages to the 20th century. The museum is housed in the Hôtel de Saint-Aignan, a beautiful 17th-century building
located in the middle of Le Marais where many Jews lived before the mass deportations during the Second World War.
In addition to religious artefacts and richly embroidered garments from previous eras, this is a good place to see work
by renowned artists such as Modigliani, Soutine, Lipchitz and Boltanski. The Museum also houses the archive of the
Dreyfus Affair, an important resource for anyone researching the pernicious impact of 19th-century anti-semitism.

Musée de la Vie Romantique

Hôtel Scheffer-Renan, 16 rue Chaptal, 75009 ☎ 01 55 31 95 67
Free for permanent exhibition **€** for temporary exhibitions
www.paris.fr **Open** every day 10am–6pm, closed Monday and public holidays
Métro Saint-Georges, Pigalle, Blanche, Liège **Bus** 67, 68, 74, 30
Only the garden and the workshops are accessible, not the main house. Tactile visits with a talk are given to partially sighted visitors amd the museum also offers guided tours for people with learning difficulties

Although the idea of Romanticism sounds a little frivolous, this museum offers a fascinating insight into the lives of 19th-century literary figures. Housed in a grand villa formerly owned by the Dutch artist Ary Schaffer, the setting feels surprisingly rural. Wandering around restored period rooms you might come across some unexpected and revealing objects. In one glass case the plaster cast of the writer George Sand's arm can still be seen – perhaps she held hands with Chopin walking round the small but delightful garden. An enticing tea room in the conservatory is open from mid-April to mid-October, serving tisanes, coffee, light lunches and pastries.

Libraries

Bibliothèque Chaptal

26 rue Chaptal, 75009 ☎ 01 49 70 92 80
Free
Open Tuesday, Thursday, Friday 1pm–7pm, Wednesday
10am–7pm, Saturday 10am–6pm, closed Monday, Sunday
and public holidays
Métro Blanche **Bus** 67, 68, 74
There is access for wheelchair users and an adapted toilet

This really beautiful public library is a delight for both younger
and older readers. It is a utopian place, combining the elegance
of the 18th century with the colourful, optimistic interior design
of today. The enlightenment ideals are epitomised in having
access to thousands of fascinating publications, from French
literature to history books and travel guides. The enchanting
drawing room with its ornate mirror and painted ceilings is still
a comfortable place to read a daily (French) paper or leaf through
the illustrated books on the open shelves.

La Fondation Custodia, Collection Fritz Lugt

Institut Neerlandais, 121 rue de Lille, 75007 ☎ 01 47 05 75 19
Free www.fondationcustodia.fr **Open** Monday–Friday 10am–1pm for study by appointment (contact turgot@
fondationcustodia.fr), guided tours are offered once a month and last 1 hour (contact coll.lugt@fondationcustodia.fr)
Métro Assemblée Nationale **Bus** 24, 63, 69, 73, 83, 84, 94
The foundation is wheelchair accessible, except for the staircase leading to the first floor

At the rear of the Institut Neerlandais lies what is probably the quietest drawing room in Paris. L'Hôtel Turgot is not only one of the most elegant villas in the city, it also houses a superlative collection of art from the 15th to the 20th century. The Custodia Foundation was created in 1947 by the Dutch businessman Fritz Lugt to manage the many artworks and historical documents he'd amassed over the years. With over 90,000 objects, including etchings, rare prints, oil paintings, marble busts, watercolour landscapes and antique furniture, this is an exceptional collection. Among the outstanding pieces are a red chalk drawing of a woman by Peter Paul Rubens, a portrait by Albrecht Dürer and numerous etchings by Rembrandt van Rijn.

Bibliothèque / Vidéothèque Roméo Martinez, Maison Européenne de la Photographie

5–7 rue de Fourcy, 75004 ☎ 01 44 78 75 00 for the main desk, 01 44 78 75 44 for the library
€ but free on Wednesday after 5pm
www.mep-fr.org
Open Wednesday–Sunday 11am–8pm, closed Monday, Tuesday, public holidays, and from mid-July to mid-August
Métro Saint Paul, Pont Marie **Bus** 67, 69, 76, 96
There is wheelchair access to the library and the exhibition spaces – ask at the entrance desk for the (very slow) staff lift

The exhibitions here are exceptionally varied, but, as the name suggests, this extensive library collection focuses on European photography. You might come to see the secret photo albums of the actress Charlotte Rampling but then find yourself entranced by a compilation of Paul Thorel's evocative black and white portraits glimpsed on another shelf. Although school parties may interrupt the calm in the main galleries upstairs, the library remains a quiet space to peruse photobooks and periodicals in this handsome 300-year-old mansion.

The American Library in Paris

10 rue du Général Camou, 75007 ☎ 01 53 59 12 60
€ www.americanlibraryinparis.org **Open** Tuesday–
Saturday 10am–7pm, Sunday 1pm–7pm, closed most
public holidays **Métro** Ecole Militaire, Alma-Marceau
RER Pont de l'Alma **Bus** 42, 63, 69, 80, 82, 87, 92
There is disabled access to two of the three library floors

This independent library was established over 90 years
ago to provide study space and support to both American
students and families living in Paris and its dual role
continues to this day. There are comfortable sofas to curl up
with a novel, a glass-walled space for book groups to meet,
and plenty of magazines to browse if you are just dropping by.

Bibliothèque de la Maison de Victor Hugo

Hôtel de Rohan-Guéménée, 6 place des Vosges, 75004
☎ 01 42 72 10 16 **Free** www.paris.fr **Open** Monday–Friday
10am–12.30pm and 2pm–5.30pm, closed public holidays
Métro Bastille, Chemin Vert **Bus** 20, 29, 69, 76, 96
There is access for wheelchair users

The novelist Victor Hugo lived in this grand, second floor
apartment from 1832 to 1848 and wrote many of his famous
novels here in the heart of Paris. At the start of the 20th
century it was turned into a museum and many of Hugo's
original texts and drawings survive intact, including
hundreds of handwritten manuscripts. This is a fascinating
library for anyone interested in Hugo's life and work.

Bibliothèque Fondation Custodia / Centre Culturel des Pays-Bas

121 rue de Lille, 75007 ☎ 01 53 59 12 40 **Free** to use the reference library
www.institutneerlandais.com
Open Monday 1pm–9pm, Tuesday–Friday 1pm–7pm, exhibitions Tuesday–Sunday 1pm–7pm
Métro Assemblée Nationale **RER** Invalides, Musée d'Orsay **Bus** 63, 73, 83, 94
The library and the exhibition space are both accessible for wheelchair users

The reading room of the Institut Néerlandais / Fondation Custodia (The Netherlands Cultural Centre) may not be large, but this is a very civilised place to carry out art historical research. The library has one of the largest and most important art history collections in France and includes contemporary monographs and catalogues as well as books on art from previous eras and is open to everyone. As well as bound publications, the collection also holds many precious documents such as Indian miniatures and handwritten letters by Gauguin and Manet (viewed by appointment). You might find yourself sharing a table with a curator of antiquities or a local artist curious to read the latest edition of an international art journal.

Bibliothèque Sainte Geneviève

10 place du Panthéon, 75005
☎ 01 44 41 97 97
Free www-bsg.univ-paris1.fr
Open Monday–Saturday 10am–10pm, closed
for student vacations
Métro Cardinal Lemoine, Maubert Mutualité,
Cluny-La Sorbonne **RER** Luxembourg
Bus 21, 27, 47, 84, 89
Wheelchair users should call 01 44 41 97 74
one day in advance for assistance (to be
guided to an alternative entrance)

Imagine a huge reading room with curved
iron roof braces in the style of the Eiffel
Tower and you'll get a good impression of
this magnificent 19th-century library. In fact,
this was the architectural project Gustave
Eiffel was commissioned to design just prior
to his more famous Parisian landmark.
The Saint Geneviève University Library has
been described as encyclopaedic and it is
hard to argue with this one word description.
Even if you don't intend to carry out research
in the stunning Labrouste reading room,
guided tours (in French) are possible in
small groups. You can also visit on your own
between 9am and 10am in the morning on
the days it is open. Bring a passport or
other form of ID to obtain a reader's card.

Bibliothèque Marguerite Durand

9 rue Nationale, 75013 ☎ 01 53 82 76 77
Free www.paris.fr
Open Tuesday–Saturday 2pm–6pm, closed on public holidays
Métro Métro Olympiades, Porte d'Ivry **Bus** 27, 62, 64, 83
There is access for wheelchair users via a small lift

This little-known library on women's lives and achievements fills the mezzanine of a modern public library near to Place d'Italie. Founded in 1932 thanks to the generous donation of the feminist journalist Marguerite Durand (1864–1936) to the city of Paris, the library is an excellent resource for anyone interested in the history of French women and feminism. Not only will you find complete editions of *La Fronde*, her feminist daily newspaper, in the archives, but also contemporary art magazines and feminist journals in French and English. From Janine Niepce's original black and white photographs of Colette and Simone de Beauvoir to filmed footage of street protests in the 1970s, this is an excellent centre for delving into the archives of women's history.

Centre Culturel Irlandais

5 rue des Irlandais, 75005 ☎ 01 58 52 10 30,
01 58 52 10 83 for the library
Free www.centreculturelirlandais.com
Open exhibition space Tuesday–Saturday
2pm–6pm, Wednesday until 8pm, Sunday
12.30pm–2.30pm, closed Monday and public
holidays. Médiathèque open Monday–Friday
2pm–6pm, Wednesday until 8pm, closed
weekends and public holidays
Métro Place Monge **RER** Luxembourg,
Cardinal Lemoine **Bus** 21, 27, 84
There is access for wheelchair users to the
médiathèque and garden

There are two libraries in this handsome
18th-century building: the Old Library of
the Irish College, built around 1775, above
Saint Patrick's chapel, and the modern
Médiathèque, which is open to anyone
curious about Irish literature, film, history
and culture. In addition to DVDs, books in
Gaelic and publications on contemporary
Ireland, there are a few magazines, such
as one on Irish archaeology, the art
journal *Circa* and *Poetry Ireland Review*.
Monographs on artists such as Anne
Tallentire can be found on the shelves as
well as the collected works of Oscar Wilde,
a former resident of the city.

Bibliothèque Forney

Hotel de Sens, 1 rue du Figuier, 75004
☎ 01 42 78 14 60
Free bring ID, proof of address and a recent photograph for a library pass
www.paris.fr
Open Tuesday, Friday, Saturday 1pm–7.30pm, Wednesday, Thursday 10am–7.30pm, closed Sunday, Monday and public holidays
Métro Pont-Marie, Saint-Paul **Bus** 67
There is no access for wheelchairs to the library

This wonderful art and design library was founded by the forward-looking industrialist Samuel-Aimé Forney in 1886. Intended primarily as a resource for graphic design, textiles and advertising apprentices, today the library welcomes students and designers from all over France. In addition to art and design journals and over 230,000 technical manuals and books on the decorative arts, the library is also a repository for thousands of everyday documents, from original 1960s posters advertising orangina to 19th-century manufacturer's fabric samples. If you are looking for 1970s swirly turquoise patterned wallpaper for your next movie, this is the place to find it. The building is also rather fascinating – constructed in 1475, it was home to the Archbishops of Sens and is an excellent example of early Renaissance architecture. This medieval building has an exquisite formal garden, which you can reach by walking along Quai de Hôtel de Ville towards Métro Pont-Marie.

Parks and gardens

Musée Carnavalet / Histoire de Paris

23 rue de Sévigné, 75003 ☎ 01 44 59 58 58
Free for the permanent collection and gardens
€ for temporary exhibitions
www.carnavalet.paris.fr
Open Tuesday–Saturday 10am–6pm, no entry after 5pm, closed
on Monday, 1 May and other public holidays including Easter
Sunday and Pentecost
Métro Saint-Paul or Chemin Vert **Bus** 29, 69, 76, 96
The garden is accessible for wheelchair users, however many
parts of the museum are not. Use the entrance at 29 rue de
Sévigné and ring in advance to arrange access

The Museum of the History of Paris has two typical French
formal gardens – one overlooked by the Hôtel Carnavalet
and the other by the Hotel Le Peletier de Saint-Fargeau.
These handsome 18th-century buildings are the perfect
backdrop for ornate, neatly clipped low box hedges arranged
in spiral patterns. Surrounding the parterres are hydrangeas
and scented pale pink rose bushes interspersed with red
carnations and variegated green hosta. If the weather is
poor, you can always venture indoors to discover 18th-century
drawing rooms, as well as drawings by Corot and a portrait of
a rather portly looking Marie de Médicis.

Jardin Anne Frank

14 impasse Berthaud, 75003. On the corner of rue Rambuteau and rue Beauborg, the entrance to the park is next to the Musée des Poupées just after the restaurant Le Hangar

Free www.paris.fr
Open May–August daily 10am–8.30pm
Métro Rambuteau, Châtelet **Bus** 20, 38, 39, 47, 75
There is good access for wheelchair users

The area around the nearby Centre Georges Pompidou can get very crowded, making this small inner city park just off the beaten track seem even more of a secluded haven. Few tourists venture here, yet this modern garden has some pretty views of 18th-century mansions as well as a simple, circular parterre surrounded by a low box hedge. There are a few stone benches in front of leafy saplings – the overall design seems to have combined the features of a traditional formal garden with a contemporary sensibility.

Promenade Plantée

1 avenue Daumesnil, 75012 ☎ 01 42 76 40 40

€ www.paris.fr **Open** In summer (from April) weekdays 8am–8.30pm, weekends 9am–8.30pm, and to 8pm in September. In winter (until end of February) the walkway closes at 5.45pm and in March at 7pm

Métro Bastille, Ledru-Rollin **RER** Gare de Lyon **Bus** 20, 29, 57, 65, 87, 91

The planted walkway is accessible from the avenue Daumesnil by stairs and lifts with other entrances on boulevard Carnot, avenue Émile-Laurent or rue Edouard Lartet

This aerial walkway used to be a railway line from Bastille to Saint-Maur until it was decommissioned at the end of the sixties. Although it is not the quietest green space in Paris, as sounds from the main road below can still be heard high above the traffic, it is still a delightful place to go for a walk. There are even rectangular ponds up here providing safe habitats for a variety of birdlife, including breeding ducks and chirping sparrows. The vistas change every few yards as the planting has been carefully thought out to provide endless variety along the route. Seeing the white flowers of the North American Virginia bird cherry in late spring is especially heartening.

Parc André Citroën

quai André Citroën, 75015 ☎ 01 40 71 75 60 **Free** www.paris.fr
Open weekdays 8am–8.30pm, weekdends and public holidays
9am–8.30pm in summer, until dusk in winter **Métro** Javel-André
Citroën, Balard **RER** Javel, Pont de Garigliano **Bus** 42, 88, 169
The park is wheelchair accessible with adapted toilets

This modern park built on the site of the former Citroën car
factory is a spacious 14-hectare open space, overlooking the
Seine, and full of surprises: huge glasshouses towards the
south-east, smaller gardens hidden behind the long path
bordering open lawns, and, weather permitting, you can
ascend 150 metres high above the city in a helium balloon –
one of the quietest ways to see Paris from the air.

Jardin Botanique de l'Université de Paris

102 rue d'Assas, 75006 **Free** www.univ-paris5.fr/eng
Open from 15 March, guided tours from 2pm–4pm, book
48 hours in advance at jardin.botanique@pharmacie.
parisdescartes.fr. The garden is closed 1 November–
15 March **Métro** Vavin **RER** Luxembourg **Bus** 58, 82, 83
The garden is accessible for wheelchair users

This small botanic garden was created for pharmaceutical
students at the Paris Descartes University to learn about the
medicinal use of plants. Visitors are allowed to visit in spring
and summer, but it is primarily a centre for study and research.
There are over 400 species growing here, with a small pond
for aquatic flora and recently restored glasshouses.

Le Jardin de la Maison de Balzac

47 rue Raynouard 75016 ☎ 01 55 74 41 80
www.paris.fr
Free for the permanent collection and the garden **€** for temporary exhibitions
Open Tuesday–Sunday 10am–6pm, closed Monday and public holidays
Métro Passy, La Muette **RER** Radio France, Boulainvilliers **Bus** 32, 50, 70, 72
No disabled access due to the steep stairs leading down to the house and garden

This lovely small garden is perched on a hill high above the River Seine and is full of flowering bushes and lilac trees. Amongst the foliage are carved stone statues and a bust of the 19th-century writer Balzac, who lived in the adjoining villa. This must have been a delightful place for him to wander in the evening after a long day writing at his desk. Even now, it remains the ideal spot to pull up a garden chair and read a novel, especially one written by the celebrated novelist.

Parc Monceau

35 boulevard Courcelles, 75008 ☎ 01 42 27 39 56
Free www.paris.fr
Open daily 7am–10pm
Métro Monceau **Bus** 30, 94
The park is accessible for wheelchair users

This spacious city park has been appreciated by Parisians since the 18th century, and fortunately it hasn't changed much since then. The 'English style' landscaping is typical of the era and includes some intriguing follies as well as an inviting stone bridge over a small lake. There are some stunning floral displays next to the main path, covering a rocky hill with fragrant, burnt-orange wallflowers, vivid blue pansies and intricate, grey-white velvet centaurea. The semi-circle of Corinthian columns surrounding the pond is a calm place to wander, despite being named Naumachie, after a famous naval battle. The paths can get busy at the weekend, so if you want to escape the crowds, walk through the park to visit the Musee Nissim de Camondo which is both air-conditioned and almost empty.

Le Jardin du Musée Rodin

79 rue de Varenne, 75007 ☎ 01 44 18 61 10 **€** but free on the first Sunday of the month
www.musee-rodin.fr **Open** Sunday–Tuesday 10am–6pm (the garden is cleared from 5pm), closed Monday, 1 May, 25 December and 1 January, but open on other public holidays
Métro Varenne, Invalides **RER** Invalides **Bus** 69, 82, 87, 92
The garden is wheelchair accessible, but in the Hotel Miron (the museum) there are no lifts to the first floor

It is hard to believe that a garden this large and beautiful still exists in the centre of Paris. The Rodin Museum can get rather crowded but the tranquil lawns behind the villa seem to stretch on forever, making this a wonderful place to wander round in warm weather. This is probably one of the world's most sophisticated sculpture gardens: the dramatic scene of Rodin's bronze of two men locked in perpetual battle in the middle of a round pond is tempered by the tall green hedge behind, whilst elsewhere his monumental *Gates of Hell* acts as a vivid memento mori. Opposite this sculpture, a diminutive Eiffel Tower can just be seen behind his trio of naked, bronze male figures. In summer the surrounding rose bushes are in full bloom, making this a very attractive place for rosarians as well as art lovers.

Cimetière du Montparnasse

3 boulevard Edouard Quinet, 75014 ☎ 01 44 10 86 50
Free www.parisinfo.com **Open** in summer Monday–
Saturday 8.30am–6pm, Sunday 9am–6pm, in winter
Monday–Saturday 8am–5.30pm, Sunday 9am–5.30pm
Métro Edgar Quinet, Raspail, Montparnasse-Bienvenue
RER Montparnasse-Bienvenue **Bus** 28, 68
There is access for wheelchair users

This simply laid out cemetery is not only a good place
to pay one's respects to the famous (including Samuel
Beckett, Simone de Beauvoir and Jean-Paul Sartre), it is
also a lovely spot to sit under the maple trees – the pace of
life is slow and gentle in this calm corner of the city.

Le Potager des Oiseaux

rue des Oiseaux, 75003 ☎ 06 17 87 66 72 **Free**
www.jardinons-ensemble.org **Open** Saturday, Sunday
10am–1pm, for an appointment to visit contact Bruno
Charenton at bruenho@free.fr
Métro Arts et Métiers, Rambuteau, Temple **Bus** 20, 75, 96
There is disabled access to the garden

At the back of the Marché des Enfants Rouges market is a
small gate which leads to the Potager des Oiseaux, a small
kitchen garden where amateur gardeners of all ages grow
herbs and vegetables in neat rows inside wooden-framed
plots. In the autumn everyone shares their harvested
produce during convivial communal meals.

Jardins Francs-Bourgeois-Rosiers

31 rue des Francs Bourgeois, 75004. The entrance to the garden is to the right of the welcome desk
of the Maison De L'Europe, at the far left corner of the courtyard
Free www.paris.fr
Open every day 2pm until dusk
Métro Saint-Paul, Chemin-Vert **Bus** 29, 96
There is one step into the garden, making it difficult for wheelchair users to enter without assistance

Although it is called the Garden of Roses, there is mainly one lawn here, surrounded by straight paths, a few wooden
benches, and tall maize plants. The pretty, diminutive silver birch trees in the centre of the garden are the main
attraction, as well as the fact that this is a really tranquil, sunny spot away from the fashionable backstreets in busy
Le Marais. There didn't seem to be many roses visible during early summer, but these may flourish at other times of
the year.

Les Jardins des Archives Nationales

60 rue Francs Bourgeois, 75003 ☎ 01 40 27 61 20 for general enquiries, 01 40 27 62 18 for guided visits
Free www.archivesnationales.culture.gouv.fr/chan/chan/musee/jardins-archives-paris.html
Open every day May–October 8am–7pm, November–April 8am–5pm
Métro Rambuteau, Hôtel de Ville **Bus** 29, 75
The paths are accessible to wheelchair users

There are four gardens surrounding the monumental buildings which house France's national archives. After entering the main courtyard with its stone benches and formal, cone-shaped box topiary, walk through the passage on the right to find the four hidden gardens with small ponds, huge plane trees and lilac bushes. One of these, the garden of the Hôtel de Rohan, has tall pines and a few wooden benches to sit on warm days. When the weather is cooler, follow the lavender bordered path in the modern Jardin de l'Hôtel de Fontenay, then stroll past the rare Indian chestnut tree in the more wooded grounds on the left.

Jardin Atlantique

1 place des Cinq Martyrs du Lycée Buffon, 75015
☎ 01 40 64 39 44
Free www.paris.fr
Open weekdays 8am–9.30pm, weekends and
public holidays 9am–9.30pm. Guided tours can be
arranged through the Direction des Parcs et Jardins
located at 1 avenue Gordon Bennett, 75016
Métro Montparnasse-Bienvenue
RER Montparnasse **Bus** 91, 92, 94, 95, 96
The garden is wheelchair accessible – there is a
public lift to the right of the station on the boulevard
de Vaurigard

Some inspired Parisian town planner in the early
1990s was imaginative enough to come up with
the idea of planting a garden on top of the busy
Montparnasse railway station. Named after the
fact that the trains beneath mainly take travellers
to destinations on the Atlantic coast, this is a
delightful place to sit on the grass or find a quiet
corner to read a book. There are spacious lawns, a
narrow gravelled area to play boules and a secret,
'silent wall' made of irregular shaped stones near
to the maze-like wooden walkways. The colourful
herbaceous border makes a particularly attractive
entrance to this rooftop garden.

Square Georges Cain

8 rue Payenne, 75003
Free www.paris.fr **Open** weekdays 8am–8.30pm, Saturday
and Sunday 9am–8.30pm **Métro** Saint Paul **Bus** 69, 76, 96
The garden is accessible for wheelchair users

This lovely square in the middle of Le Marais has several
carved ancient monuments at its entrance. In the centre
of the square a naked 17th-century bronze woman waits
expectantly while birds come to perch on her sculpted head.
Behind her, a row of beech trees offer a leafy backdrop for an
al fresco lunch on the picnic table. As you enter the garden,
listen out for the curious Aeolian mechanical nightingale,
whose dulcet tones can be heard whenever the wind blows.

Le Jardin de L'Hôpital St Louis

1 avenue Claude-Vellefaux, 75010, with entrances on rue
de la Grange aux Belles and rue Bichat **Free** www.paris.fr
Open May–October, Sunday 11am–5pm **Métro** Colonel
Fabien, Goncourt **RER** Gare de L'Est **Bus** 46, 75
The hospital garden is accessible to wheelchair users

On the order of King Henri IV, the Hospital Saint Louis was
built in Paris and completed in 1612. Eight years later, apricot
and almond trees were planted in the garden and the sale
of their fruits raised money for the upkeep of the hospital.
Many of the original buildings survive and this is still a calm,
verdant place to wander, four hundred years after the first
patients looked out at the peaceful quadrangle.

Parc de Bercy

128 quai de Bercy, 75012, with entrances on rue Paul-Belmondo, rue Joseph-Kessel, rue de l'Ambroisie, rue François-Truffaut, quai, boulevard et rue de Bercy, rue de Cognac, rue de Pommard, cour Chamonard
Free (€ for weekend gardening courses) www.paris.fr
Open May–August Monday–Friday 8am–9.30pm, Saturday and Sunday 9am–9.30pm
Métro Cour Saint-Émilion, Bercy **RER** Bibliothèque François Mitterand **Bus** 24, 64, 87
The park is wheelchair accessible but the gardening library is at the top of a flights of stairs in La Maison du Jardinage

This modern park on the edge of the city is full of surprises. From the picturesque ruins near the cour Saint-Emilion entrance to the wooden log 'hotel' for flying insects, there is plenty to see during an afternoon ramble. The highlights of the park are the gardening school with its diminutive glasshouse and specialist library and the large kitchen garden used to teach horticultural students how to grow vegetables. There is a very realistic looking scarecrow standing in the cabbage plot – forever immobile and very, very quiet.

Le Jardin du Musée du Montmartre

12 rue Cortot, 75018 **€** www.museedemontmartre.fr
Open every day 10am–6pm **Métro** Lamarck-Caulaincourt,
Abbesses **Bus** 80 or the Montmartrobus
Most of the garden has disabled access, except for the
terrace leading down behind the museum

Avoid the crowds streaming past en route to the Sacré
Coeur Basilica and slip into this walled museum garden
located in a quiet backstreet. Instead of taking the gaudy
(and very noisy) mini-diesel train ride round the area, walk
up rue Lepic to discover the garden enjoyed by Suzanne
Valadon, August Renoir and other 19th-century artists who
initially made the village of Montmartre a bohemian centre.

UNESCO Garden of Peace

7 place de Fontenoy, 75007 **☎** 01 45 68 10 00
Free www.unesco.org/visit/jardin/fra/jardin.htm
Open weekdays 10am–6pm, closed weekends and public
holidays **Métro** Segur, Cambronne **Bus** 28, 80, 87
The garden is not easily accessed by wheelchairs

Designed by the renowned sculptor Isamu Noguchi, this
beautifully laid out Japanese garden is a real haven in the
centre of Paris. In spring the garden is a living cloud of pink
when the cherry trees are in blossom around the carp-filled
pond. Offering numerous vistas, there are many places to
sit, with views of standing stones set amongst large white
pebbles and variegated bamboo by a miniature waterfall.

Jardin du Port de l'Arsenal (Bassin de l'Arsenal)

53 boulevard de la Bastille, 75012
Free www.paris.fr
Open in summer, daily 8am–11pm **Métro** Quai de La Râpée, Bastille **Bus** 20, 29, 65, 69, 76, 86, 87, 91
There is access for wheelchairs along the paths but steps at one entrance

Arriving at the busy Bastille intersection, it's hard to imagine that only a few minutes' walk away there's a pleasant terraced waterside park alongside the Port de Plaisance de Paris Arsenal. Walking along the banks there are good views of the harbour, which was created in 1805 but is now used to berth pleasure boats and some impressive looking yachts. This is a good place to practice being an unpretentious flâneur without having to dress up to impress the fashionistas. Families come here at weekends, attracted by the relaxed, congenial atmosphere – perhaps unwittingly introducing their toddlers in pushchairs to the delights of inner city calm.

Parc Buttes Chaumont

1 rue Botzaris, 75019, with entrances on rue Manin and rue de Crimée
Free www.paris.fr
Open May–October every day 7am–10pm, and until dusk in winter
Métro Buttes Chaumont, Botzaris **Bus** 26, 48, 60, 75
The paths are rather steep for wheelchair users

The spectacular hills of the Buttes Chaumont Park used to be a gypsum quarry, and the steep paths and tranquil lakes are the pleasant result of former industrial activity. Napoleon III suggested the hill be transformed into a park and it opened to the public in 1867. This undulating park still has the feel of an old-fashioned landscape, with its crumbling grottoes, dramatic waterfall, man-made cave and pretty 19th-century lampposts. Parisians come here to wander and picnic on the grass, but, despite its popularity, even on sunny days it's still possible to find a peaceful corner to enjoy the views.

Parc Clichy-Batignolles Martin Luther King

47 rue Cardinet, 75017 **Free** www.paris.fr
Open May–September Monday–Friday 8am–9.30pm,
Saturday and Sunday 9am–9.30pm
Métro Brochant **RER** Pont-Cardinet **Bus** 31, 54, 66, 74
The park and public toilets are wheelchair accessible

This well-designed, large urban park has long, straight
paths for an afternoon promenade, raised grassy banks
where you can lie and sunbathe, a lake beyond tall reeds at
the far end and plenty of tranquil areas to sit and ponder.
There's a small communal allotment full of decorated
plant pots, a shaggy scarecrow and an abundance of herbs
– usually the quietest spot in the park.

Le Jardin de L'École Normale Supérieure

45 rue d'Ulm, 75005 ☎ 01 44 32 30 00 **Free** www.ens.fr
Open from mid-September daily 9am–5pm, closed for
summer vacation **Métro** Censier-Daubenton, Place Monge
RER Luxembourg, Port-Royal **Bus** 21, 27, 47
The garden is not wheelchair accessible

One of the most prestigious higher education institutions in
the world has a secret garden where a few students come
to find a quiet place to read. Although the lawn looks a bit
unkempt, the trees are magnificent – a venerable yew and
huge chestnuts provide welcome shade in the summer. Enter
by the porter's lodge on rue d'Ulm, and the garden is on the
left, surrounded by 18th-century villas and college buildings.

Fondation Cartier Pour L'Art Contemporain

261 boulevard Raspail, 75014 ☎ 01 42 18 56 50
€ but free entry on Wednesday from 2pm–6pm, and to the garden
www.fondation.cartier.fr **Open** Tuesday 11am–10pm Wednesday–Sunday 11am–8pm, closed Monday, 25 December,
1 January but open other public holidays
Métro Raspail, Denfert-Rochereau **RER** Denfert-Rochereau **Bus** 38, 68, 91
The garden and the building are both wheelchair accessible

The Cartier Foundation for Contemporary Art not only hosts inspiring, beautifully presented temporary exhibitions from around the world, it also has a very enticing 'jardin sauvage'. Wild flowers from all over France were planted here after architect Jean Nouvel's glass-walled building was completed in 1994. His transparent structure is meant to blur the distinction between interior and exterior and one corner of the building was even built to accommodate a revered 200-year-old Cedar of Lebanon. Here, it seems, nature has the upper hand. There is also an excellent art bookshop on the first floor for when the weather is less clement.

Musée de la Sculpture en Plein Air

2 quai Saint-Bernard, 75005 **Free**
Open all day, every day **Métro** Quai de la Rapée
RER Gare D'Austerlitz **Bus** 24, 63, 89
There are steps at the entrance to the sculpture garden
so it isn't accessible for wheelchair users

This wonderful open air sculpture museum along the
banks of the Seine was created in the 1980s. Instead of
neat lawns, this sculpture garden has over fifty pieces,
including work by Constantin Brâncusi and Jean Arp as
well as many less well-known artists, making this a great
place for even knowledgeable art lovers to discover some
fascinating artworks rarely seen elsewhere.

Le Jardin Partagé au Clos des Blancs Manteaux

21 rue des Blancs Manteaux, 75004 ☎ 01 71 28 50 56 **Free**
Open November–February weekends 10am–12.30pm and
1.30pm–5pm, to 5.30pm in October and March and to
6.30pm from April–September
Métro Rambuteau, Saint-Paul **Bus** 29, 75
There are steps leading to the garden so access is limited

This impressive 'jardin partagé' (shared garden) is full of
incredibly prolific plants and it's hard to believe they thrive
so well in the confines of a Parisian courtyard. The local
gardeners often organise activities here, but if you are feeling
languid, there are also a few benches to just sit and appreciate
the vigorous bay trees.

Places to relax

L'Echappée

64 rue de la Folie-Méricourt, 75011 ☎ 01 58 30 12 50
€ www.lechappee.com/spa-paris-11
Open Monday, Friday 11am–9pm, Wednesday, Thursday 11am–
11pm, Saturday, Sunday 10am–7pm, closed Tuesday. Visitors
must be aged 16 or older and there are women only sessions on
Wednesday and Thursday
Métro Oberkampf, Parmentier **Bus** 46, 56, 96
There is a lift and good access for wheelchair users to the
changing rooms, main plunge pool and ground floor treatment
rooms but not the basement

L'Echappée means 'the retreat' and once inside this
sophisticated spa, it feels as if you are far removed from
the clamour of urban life. Larger than many Parisian health
centres, the almost monochrome interior design is subdued yet
urbane. Ask for a reflexology treatment here; it is sublime – the
subtle, tender movements around one's feet and ankles are
indescribably beautiful.

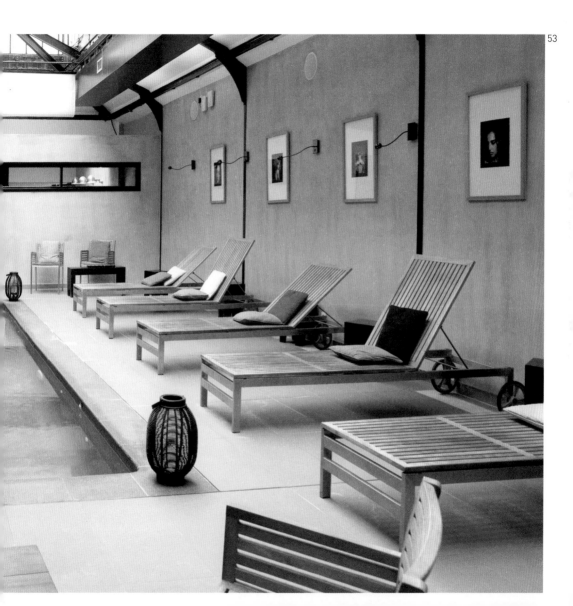

L'Espace Privé Cinq Mondes

6 square de l'Opéra Louis Jouvet, 75009 ☎ 01 42 66 00 60
€ www.cinqmondes.com
Open Monday–Wednesday 11am–8pm, Thursday to 10pm, Friday, Saturday 9am–8pm, treatments available
Monday–Saturday from 12pm, closed on public holidays
Métro Havre-Caumartin, Madeleine, Opéra **RER** Auber **Bus** 20, 21, 22, 27, 29, 53, 52, 66, 68, 81, 95
There is no disabled access to the treatment rooms

From a typical 19th-century Parisian street near to the opera, it's hard to imagine the soothing interior of this chic spa. Treat yourself to a warm bath filled with fresh rose petals and the delicate aroma of essential oils, followed by an invigorating hot stone massage. Whether you are an office worker tired of being slumped behind a computer or just visiting this rather grand part of the city, the Cinq Mondes spa is the perfect place for your body to receive expert care and attention. All the beauty products used here are paraben-free, making this an even more attractive place to unwind and relax.

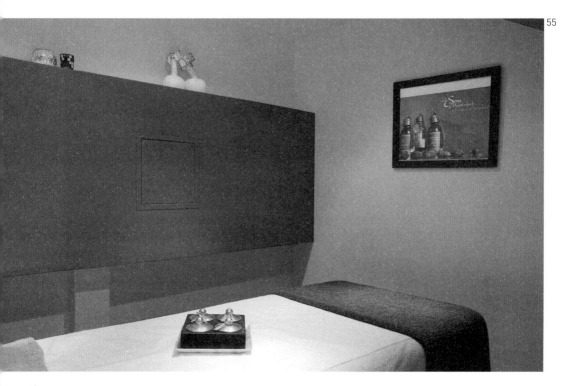

Bien Être et Spa
115 boulevard Voltaire, 75011 ☎ 01 43 48 40 87
€ www.bienetreetspa.fr
Open Tuesday–Sunday 10am–8pm
Métro Voltaire, Charonne **Bus** 46, 56, 76
There is no disabled access to the basement treatment rooms

The hammam in this city spa is so tiny there's only room for two or three people at any one time. Despite its diminutive size, however, the treatments are excellent (bring your swimming costume to wear in the hammam). Choose from four different essential oils; orange flower, verveine, ambre musk and jasmin, depending on your mood. You can tell that the young woman who works here enjoys giving massages – her happiness is infectious. If you are feeling fit you could also book yourself in for an aquabike session – but you might want to turn off the television in your personal cabin.

Buddhist Centre Kalachakra
5 passage Delessert, 75010 ☎ 01 40 05 02 22
Free (€ for breathing exercise classes and retreats) www.centre-kalachakra.com
Open every day 2pm–7pm, closed in August, guided meditation Wednesday 7.30pm
Metro Landon, Louis Blanc, Gare de L'Est **Bus** 46, 75
There is a small step into the building and a small ground floor toilet, but the doors are wide enough for a wheelchair

Every week up to a hundred people meet to practice Buddhist meditation in one large room, so it can tend to feel a bit crowded. Once the session begins, however, devotees forget their surroundings and focus on trying to quieten their busy minds. You might also be tempted by the courses held here, including classes on traditional Tibetan medicine and mindfulness breathing techniques. At the weekends, locals come to sail their small wind-powered boats on the peaceful Canal St Martin nearby and it's very calming to sit and watch the gently floating yachts if you arrive a bit early. The centre also holds Buddhist retreats in rural locations during the annual summer exodus from the city.

Red Earth Yoga Centre

235 rue La Fayette, 75010 ☎ 01 40 38 40 52
€ www.redearthcentre.com
Open check the website for classes, held most days
Métro Jaurès, Louis Blanc **Bus** 26, 48
The centre is wheelchair accessible

Tucked away behind a large metal door at the back of a quiet courtyard, this small yoga centre is a very enticing, calm-inducing place. The women teachers offer meditative or dynamic forms of yoga including prenatal classes, yoga for children and gentle shiatsu massage. In one corner there are also a few books for sale on Zen meditation and Japanese gardens.

Assa Salon de Bien-être Japonais

8 rue Christine, 75006 ☎ 01 46 34 59 08
€ www.assa-spa.fr **Open** Tuesday–Sunday 11am–9pm
Métro Saint Michel, Odéon **Bus** 58, 63, 70, 84, 86, 87, 96
The centre is accessible for people with a disability but does not have a specially adapted toilet

This Japanese 'well-being' centre is sparsely decorated in traditional Eastern style, and the approach is similarly minimalist and unfussy. This is not a centre for beauty or nail treatments, but a rather special location for anyone wanting a full body shiatsu massage. Inspired by Eastern philosophy, the emphasis is on stress reduction and instilling a sense of calm. Only organic essential oils are used.

Centre Nadopasana

19 avenue de Clichy, 75017 ☎ 01 47 82 40 04
€ www.yoga-detente.com
Open classes on Tuesday and Thursday at 7.30pm and Friday at 12.30pm
Métro Place de Clichy **Bus** 30, 54, 66, 74, 80, 81, 95
The meditation and changing rooms have step-free access but there is no specially adapted toilet

Three times a week Armelle Denolle runs gentle Hatha yoga sessions in a small meditation centre near to the Place de Clichy. A very small group of students follow her guidance, making this class feel both intimate and restful. Inspired by the teachings of Sri Shyamji Bhatnagar, the class ends with a restful meditation, during which the teacher gently plays the four stringed tanpura in a room softly lit with candlelight.

Bains D'Orient

place de la bataille de Stalingrad, 75010 ☎ 01 40 05 03 90
www.lesbainsdorient.com
Open Monday–Saturday 11am–9pm, Sunday 10am–8pm
Métro Stalingrad, Jaurès **Bus** 26, 48, 54
There is no access for wheelchairs to this first floor hammam

The exterior looks rather nondescript but once inside this oriental bath house, you'll feel as if you have been transported to another world. Luxuriate in the steamy surroundings of the tiled hammam then be scrubbed with Moroccan black soap and a special kassa mitt which exfoliates dead skin and makes you feel as smooth as a baby. Follow this with a relaxing massage or a pedicure. If some of the interior seems a little scruffy, it's worth remembering that the women who work here are warm and friendly. Afterwards, wrap yourself in a towelling robe, lie down on a chaise longue and the hostess will bring you a Turkish patisserie and hot mint tea.

This centre is for women only. Bring your own bikini bottoms and flip-flops to wear in the hammam.

Coraline Genaivre, Médecine Traditionnelle Chinoise
square Claude Debussy, 75017
☎ 06 76 56 79 57, call ahead to make an appointment and for the exact address €
Métro Villiers **RER** Pont Cardinet **Bus** 30, 94, La Traverse Batignolles-Bichat
The practice is wheelchair accessible

Coraline Genaivre recently qualified as a practitioner of traditional Chinese medicine and offers reasonably priced acupuncture and moxa treatments in a well-to-do suburb in the west of Paris. Even after one treatment, clients often come away feeling a sense of calm and well-being. You don't have to have a physical complaint to make an appointment: Chinese medicine treats the whole person so helps the mind and body achieve a reciprocal harmony. Even just lying down in this quiet room talking to the sympathetic practitioner will begin to alleviate feelings of stress.

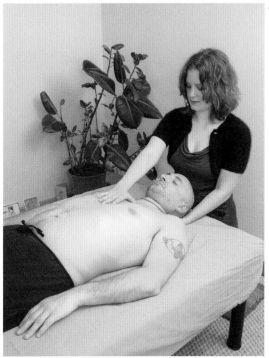

Ouse-An Massage

34 rue Pierre-Larousse, 75014 ☎ 01 45 40 02 54
€ www.ouse-an.com
Open Monday–Saturday by appointment only
Métro Plaisance **Bus** 58, 62 **Tramway** D3 to Diderot
The ground floor rooms are accessible but the toilet is not specially adapted for wheelchair users

Apparently, this is the only place in Paris where you can experience the traditional Vietnamese massage le Dam Bop Tam Quat. This centuries old technique is handed down from experts to a few initiated recipients, including Tu Minh Tan, who works in this simply decorated massage room.

Centre D'Intégration Structurelle Paris

88 rue de Buzenval 75020 ☎ 01 43 48 76 50
€ www.rolfmethodeparis.com **Open** by appointment only, evening sessions available **Métro** Buzenval, Avron **RER** Nation **Bus** 57, La Traverse de Charonne
The centre is not wheelchair accessible

Jessica Blean learnt the art of Rolfing in the United States and is one of the very few practitioners of this deep-tissue massage technique in Paris. She and her French husband Nicolas employ the techniques devised by Dr Ida Rolf developed in the early part of the twentieth century to help unlock long-held structural tension in the body. Both practitioners speak excellent English.

Places of worship

Église Saint Séverin
3 rue des Prêtres Saint-Séverin, 75005 ☎ 01 42 34 93 50
Free www.saint-severin.com
Open Monday–Saturday 11am–7.30pm, Sunday 9am–8.30pm
Mass is held on weekdays at 12.15pm and 7pm
Métro Saint Michel, Cluny-La Sorbonne **RER** Saint Michel
Bus 21, 24, 27, 38, 47, 63, 85, 86, 87
The church is wheelchair accessible

This ancient church on the Left Bank is named after a devout hermit and dates from the 11th century. It is a magnificent example of late Gothic architecture, and has unusual interior features as well as fantastic gargoyles on the roof. The twisted pillar in the shape of a palm tree is a superb example of medieval stone carving. Surrounding this sculptural column are Jean René Bazaine's vibrant stained glass windows. On sunny days they radiate vivid cobalt blue and intense red light.

Église de Notre Dame de Travail

36 rue Guilleminot 75014 ☎ 01 44 10 72 92
Free www.notredamedutravail.net
Open Monday–Saturday 10am–7.30pm (after mass), Sunday 10am–6pm
Métro Gâîté, Pernety **Bus** 91
The church has good access for wheelchair users

This extraordinary church was designed to be as welcoming as possible to the factory working population of Paris so is constructed from steel and iron girders rather than traditional stone. Jules Astuc, the architect, was probably inspired by Eiffel, the designer of the eponymous tower. The industrial interior is surprisingly inventive and this is not only a quiet church but also a historically fascinating one. The stylised flower wall paintings added in the early 1900s are good examples of the Arts and Crafts movement in an ecclesiastical setting.

Église Saint-Nicholas des Champs

254 rue Saint-Martin, 75003 ☎ 01 42 72 92 54
Free to enter but donations are welcome
www.asaintnicolas.com
Open Monday–Friday 7.45am–7.30pm (after mass),
Saturday 10.30am–1pm and 4pm–7.30pm, Sunday
9.45am–12.30pm and 4pm–6.30pm, reduced
opening hours in August
Métro Arts et Métiers, Réaumur-Sébastopol
RER Châtelet-Les Halles **Bus** 20, 38, 47
There is access for wheelchair users

This magnificent Gothic church started off as a
simple chapel in 1184 and was gradually added
to during the next 500 years. After the French
Revolution it temporarily became a secular temple
to worship Hymen and Fidelity, but the Catholic
parish took up residence again in 1802. In the 18th
century, plain glass windows were added above
simple Doric columns to lighten up the rather dark
medieval interior. Walk up rue Saint Martin, past
the small galleries and Lebanese cafés serving
hot flatbreads, to rest awhile in this venerable old
church. Weekdays mid-morning seems a quiet
time to visit as there are no services.

Centre Quaker International

114 bis rue Vaugirard, 75006 ☎ 01 45 48 74 23 **Free**
http://quaker.chez-alice.fr **Open** for worship Sunday 11am,
first and second Tuesday of the month 7pm
Métro Falguière, Duroc, Saint-Placide, Montparnasse-
Bienvenue **Bus** 28, 39, 70, 82, 89, 92
There is a lift to the basement, but also steps to negotiate

Every Sunday, Quakers, and often non-Quakers, meet for an
hour of silence in this unassuming centre south of the Seine.
There may be gentle interruptions as someone 'bears witness',
but the shared thoughts are usually insightful and prescient.
Quakers tend to be quietly welcoming and visitors are invited to
stay for a simple vegetarian lunch after meeting for worship.

Kehilat Gesher
La Communauté Juive Franco-Anglophone
7 rue Léon Cogniet, 75017 ☎ 01 39 21 97 19 **Free**
www.kehilatgesher.org **Open** for service times see
website, office open Monday–Thursday 1.30pm–6.30pm
Métro Courcelles, Wagram **Bus** 30, 81, 84
The synagogue is wheelchair accessible

This small synagogue is tucked down a back street in an
affluent district near to Parc Monceau. The liberal
French-Anglophone Jewish Community is very welcoming
to anyone living in or visiting Paris. The Rabbi also organises
interdenominational events, bridging gaps between different
faiths and cultures.

Église Saint Thomas D'Aquin

3 place Saint Thomas d'Aquin, 75007 ☎ 01 42 22 59 74
Free www.eglisesaintthomasdaquin.fr
Open weekdays 8.30am–12pm and 2.30pm–7pm, Saturday 10am–12pm and 5pm–7pm, Sunday 10am–12pm,
with reduced opening hours from mid-July to mid-August
Métro Rue du Bac, Solférino **RER** Musée D'Orsay **Bus** 63, 68, 69, 83, 84, 94
The church is wheelchair accessible

The 17th-century church of Saint Thomas D'Aquinas is an incredibly grand and imposing edifice. As well as
the architecturally impressive main nave, the walls of the church are hung with huge oil paintings depicting
dramatic scenes from the Bible. Behind the altar lies the large Saint Louis chapel, which has one of the most
spectacular painted ceilings in Paris.

Temple du Marais, Église Protestante Reformée

17 rue St Antoine, 75004 ☎ 01 42 74 40 82
Free http://temple.dumarais.fr
Open Saturday afternoon and by appointment.
Services are held throughout the week
Métro Saint Paul, Bastille, Sully Morland
Bus 20, 29, 67, 69, 76, 86, 87, 91
There is no access for wheelchair users

This exceptional Baroque building used to be the chapel for the Convent of the Visitation Saint-Marie. Built in 1632, it was modelled on the Pantheon in Rome and the ceiling is spectacular, with its 17th-century oval skylights and ornate stone carvings. The contemporary wall hangings on either side of the altar are perfectly in keeping with the old surroundings, and although this isn't the largest church in Paris, it is worth a visit to see these alone.

Église Saint-Julien-le-Pauvre

79 rue Galande, 75005 ☎ 01 43 54 52 16
Free www.sjlpmelkites.org
Open Tuesday–Sunday 9.30am–1pm and 3pm–6pm, closed Monday
Métro Saint Michel, Cluny-La Sorbonne, Maubert-Mutualité **RER** Saint Michel **Bus** 21, 24, 27, 63, 85, 86, 87
The church is accessible for wheelchair users

Saint Julian the Poor is not only one of the oldest churches in Paris, it is also one of the most beautiful. Dating from the 12th century, it has some exquisite carved stone capitals decorated with vine leaves and winged angels. Since the end of the 19th century the church has hosted the Maronite congregation and the interior is typical for Eastern Orthodox churches. Spend a few moments gazing at the beautiful iconostasis separating the nave from the ancient sanctuary.

Église Saint-Gervais

13 rue des Barres, 75004 ☎ 01 48 87 32 02 **Free**
Open weekdays 7.30am–12pm and 1pm–5.30pm, Saturday and Sunday 8.30am followed by vespers at 6pm most days
Métro Hotel de Ville, Saint-Paul, Pont Marie **Bus** 67, 69, 76, 96
There is access for wheelchair users

This ancient church is part of the worldwide Fraternités de Jersusalem, a monastic order whose mission is to encourage people to pray, especially in the inner city. One of the oldest catholic churches in Paris, construction of Saint Gervais began in the 1490s but it wasn't completed for another 134 years. The stone doorway and facade are somewhat misleading, however, as they were added much later in the 17th century. Inside, the very high arched Gothic ceiling is breathtaking, making this an exceptional place to sit and contemplate the important things in life.

Église Notre Dame des Victoires

place des Petits-Pères, 75002 ☎ 01 42 60 90 47 **Free**
www.notredamedesvictoires.com **Open** daily 7.30am–
7.30pm, mass weekdays 12.15pm and 7pm, Saturday and
Sunday 11am **Métro** Bourse **Bus** 20, 29, 39, 67, 74, 85
Steps to the entrance makes wheelchair access difficult

This rather dark and sombre church dating from the
1620s has a unique history. In the 19th century believers
flocked here to donate their ex-votos, expressions of
pious gratitude inscribed on marble plaques. Every
available wall has been covered in these modest
testaments to faith and these fragments of the lives
of others offer fascinating, if poignant, reading.

Église Saint Eugène et Cécile

4 rue du Conservatoire, 75009 ☎ 01 48 24 70 25 **Free**
www.saint-eugene.net **Open** Monday, Wednesday, Friday
6pm–8pm, Tuesday, Thursday 12.30pm–1.30pm in summer,
and around 2.30pm–6pm the rest of the year. Hours can
vary so ring in advance of your visit **Métro** Cadet, Grands
Boulevards, Bonne Nouvelle **Bus** 20, 32, 39, 48
There is wheelchair access, except for the spiral staircase

The cast-iron Gothic-inspired structure of this 19th-
century Catholic church is very striking. The interior is
a space to marvel at – mustard-coloured walls, green
pillars and an intricate wooden lectern. This unusual
church is where Jules Verne chose to get married.

Shops

Marie Mercié

23 rue Saint-Sulpice, 75006 ☎ 01 43 26 45 83
www.mariemercie.com
Open Tuesday–Saturday 11am–7pm, closed on public holidays
Métro Odeon, Mabillon, Saint-Sulpice **Bus** 58, 63, 70, 86, 87, 96
Disabled access is not possible as there is a step at the entrance

Marie Mercié is a fashion designer with a difference – her
extraordinary natural-straw hats are actually surreal sculptures
to be worn on the head. Imagine yourself going to the races
with a vivid orange lobster or a woven plate of trompe l'oeil fruit
balanced on top of your coiffed hair. You'll also find more sedate,
large-brimmed, pale summer hats, but if you are adventurous,
wearing Miss Mercié's perfectly proportioned black-straw hand
(with straw diamond ring) would make Salvador Dali feel very
proud.

Marie Mercié's boss, the chapelier Antony Peto, also has a
hat shop for men just outside Le Marais (www.anthonypeto.com).

Antiq Photo

16 rue de Vaugirard, 75006 ☎ 01 46 33 83 27
www.antiq-photo.com
Open Tuesday–Saturday 12pm–7pm or by appointment
Métro Cluny-La Sorbonne, Odéon
RER Luxembourg **Bus** 58, 84, 89
There is access for wheelchairs but the shop is full
of antique equipment which makes it difficult to
manoeuvre

The shelves in this narrow shop are laden with
fascinating antique photography equipment, from
framed daguerreotypes and brass magic lanterns to
heavy wooden cameras. It has the romantic feel of a
slightly neglected museum but here everything is for
sale, including working 19th-century zoetropes and
other optical illusion toys. The simple stereoscopes
with their silent, twin images are a salient reminder
that human beings once lived without cinema or
the hurried thrills of digital immediacy.

L'Atelier

58 rue Lepic, 75018 ☎ 01 42 23 96 61
www.chaussures-latelier.com
Open Tuesday–Friday 11am–1pm and 3.15pm–7.15pm, Saturday 11am–1pm and 3.15pm–6.30pm
Métro Blanche, Lamarck-Caulaincourt **Bus** 80, 95, Montmartrobus
There is limited disabled access to the small shop due to a small step at the entrance but Karim will assist anyone wanting to have a fitting

This small boutique is like an Aladdin's bazaar for the feet. Parisian men and women come here not only for the colourful prêt-a-porter boots, sandals and bags, but also for the unrivaled attention when choosing made-to-measure shoes. Karim, the imaginative shoemaker, can conjure up some beautiful designs that make chain-store shoes look rather dull. You might have to be patient for a couple of weeks while your first pair are being completed, but with the knowledge that your extremities will be adorned with hand-sewn footwear, it will be well worth the wait.

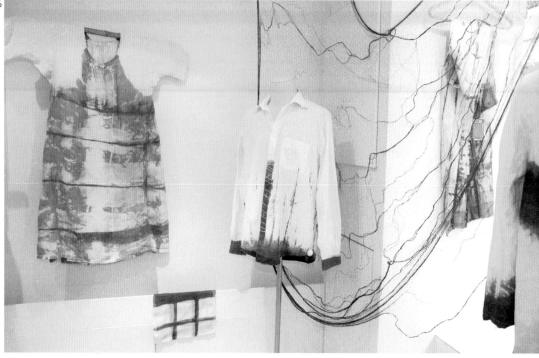

La Boutique Extraordinaire
67 rue Charlot, 75003 ☎ 01 57 40 68 85
www.laboutiqueextraordinaire.com **Open** Tuesday–Saturday 11am–8pm, Sunday 3pm–7pm
Métro Filles du Calvaire, Republique, Oberkampf **Bus** 20, 29, 65, 75, 96
The shop is wheelchair accessible

Narrow, characterful rue Charlot is full of small shops where the person behind the till is most probably the designer and maker, too. Amongst this urban profusion of inventiveness is a small boutique selling the most ravishing garments for women. If you yearn for the softest tangerine-orange cashmere jumper or a finely spun, moss-green hemp scarf, this is one of the loveliest shops in Paris. It is very rare to find clothing shops that don't play music but Agnes Butor, the warm, knowledgeable owner, not only ensures a calm atmosphere, she also hosts small exhibitions of unusual garments. You might find a hand-dipped indigo upcycled antique nightdress or a warm felted jacket that moulds itself to your body after being worn few times. Aficionados come here from as far afield as the United States and Japan – not to gawp at well-known brands but to find some of the loveliest clothes in the world.

ennelier Art Supplies

quai Voltaire, 75007 ☎ 01 42 60 72 15
ww.magasinsennelier.com **Open** Monday 2pm–6.30pm,
esday–Saturday 10am–12.45pm and 2pm–6.30pm
étro Saint Germain des Près, Rue du Bac,
lais Royal-Musée du Louvre **Bus** 27, 39, 68, 69, 95
e ground floor of the shop is wheelchair accessible

ening the drawers of soft pastels in this revered institution
like going back in time – perhaps you'll find Sennelier's
ry own 'Orange de Chine' or 'Rose Corail' among the trays
beautiful colours. In addition to their own pigments they
so stock well-known brands such as Golden and Rowney
well as exquisite papers, ink pens and brushes.

La Maison du Pastel

20 rue Rambuteau, 75003 ☎ 01 40 29 00 67
www.lamaisondupastel.com **Open** Thursday 2pm–6pm,
closed on public holidays, it is worth calling ahead to
check they are open **Métro** Rambuteau **Bus** 29, 38, 47, 75
The shop is accessible for people with a disability

Isabelle Roché continues the centuries-old tradition of
making pastels by hand in this workshop at the back of a
quiet, unassuming courtyard in Les Halles. La Maison du
Pastel is renowned for being the oldest pastel manufacturer
in the world. It can be hard to choose from their 650 colours
but seeing their neatly laid out cobalt blues or subtle greens
displayed in old-fashioned drawers is awe-inspiring.

Tzuri Gueta

1 avenue Daumesnil, 75012 ☎ 01 43 58 56 03
www.tzurigueta.com
Open Monday–Friday 9am–1pm and 2pm–7pm, Saturday 11am–7pm, closed on public holidays
Métro Bastille, Gare de Lyon **Bus** 20, 29, 57, 61, 65, 87, 91
The shop is accessible for wheelchair users

After graduating in textile engineering over a decade ago, Tzuri Gueta left his native Israel and came to work with celebrated fashion designers in Paris. He patented his unique method of using silicone to produce soft, flexible jewelle and his work has been in demand ever since. This semi-circular gallery in the Viaduc des Arts is the perfect showcase for his extraordinary creations. You'll find bunches of delicate, semi-translucent, pale blue grape-like bead necklaces just waiting to be worn around an elegant neck. Intricate white sculptures inspired by coral reefs and sea creatures hang on dark panels; their supple tentacles longing to be fondled. If you are lucky, you might get to see the workshop behind the gallery, but even if he's not there, Tzuri Gueta's wearable artworks are still worth making a detour for.

Deyrolle

6 rue de Bac, 75007 ☎ 01 42 22 30 07

www.deyrolle.com/magazine

Open Monday 10am–1pm and 2pm–7pm, Tuesday–Friday 10am–7am, closed Saturday and Sunday

Métro Rue du Bac **Bus** 63, 68, 69, 83, 84, 94

There is only wheelchair access to the ground floor

It is hard to decide whether this is a shop, a natural history museum or an amazing menagerie. Even if you can't afford a young zebra or a flying white owl, it's still worth going to see this extraordinary collection of stuffed animals. Deyrolle have been carrying out taxidermy for over 180 years and are world renowned experts in the craft. In some ways coming here is even better than visiting a zoo, because the animals don't run away and are exceptionally quiet. At the back of the building you can search through old botanical and biology prints rescued from French classrooms and check out the recently published children's books on the animal kingdom.

Artisanat Monastique

68 bis avenue Denfert Rochereau, 75014 ☎ 01 43 35 15 76
www.artisanatmonastique.com **Open** Monday–Thursday
12pm–7pm, Saturday 2pm–7pm **Métro** Port Royal,
Denfert Rocherau **RER** Port Royal **Bus** 38, 83, 91
Disabled access to the ground floor only

This is a good place to visit in the summer as most of the
rooms are located in the cool, converted cellars of an ancient
monastery. You can do a rather special shop here – from cold
pressed olive oil, delicately scented soap, furniture polish,
home-made jams and fruit liqueurs to bridesmaid's outfits
and hand-knitted children's cardigans. All the high quality
products are made by nuns or monks in thriving monasteries.

Au Dela des Frontières

106 rue Amelot, 75011 ☎ 01 48 06 85 04
www.audeladesfrontieres.com **Open** Tuesday–Friday
12pm–3pm and 5pm–8pm, Saturday 12pm–8pm, closed
Sunday **Métro** Filles du Calvaire, Oberkampf **Bus** 20, 65, 96
The shop has access for wheelchair users

The name of this fair trade shop translates as 'Beyond
Borders', and the owner insists that not only is it important
to sell goods from developing economies, but also for people
to re-think the imaginary borders in their own minds. The
music-free environment makes it possible to quietly appreciate
craft items, from brightly coloured baskets to soft silk scarves
– ideal presents for friends with a social conscience.

u Petit Bonheur La Chance

rue Saint-Paul, 75004 ☎ 01 42 74 36 38
ww.levillagesaintpaul.com
pen Thursday–Monday 11am–1.30pm and 2.30pm–7pm
étro Saint-Paul, Pont Marie **Bus** 67, 69, 76
o disabled access, as the shop is rather full of things to buy

his small shop in the village Saint Paul is filled to the ceiling with hundreds of nostalgic things from the 1920s to
e 1970s. Search inside drawers to find 30-year-old wedding cards with a pop-up bride and groom inside, or reach up
r Snow White figurines and boxes piled high with pastel-coloured, pure silk flowers. This is a vintage treasure trove to
spire imaginative amateur fashion designers or lovers of enamel blue kitchenware, and is much more enticing than
e predictable haberdashery or crockery sections of crowded department stores. Most things here are very cheap,
o – an ideal place to bring quiet children to spend their pocket money.

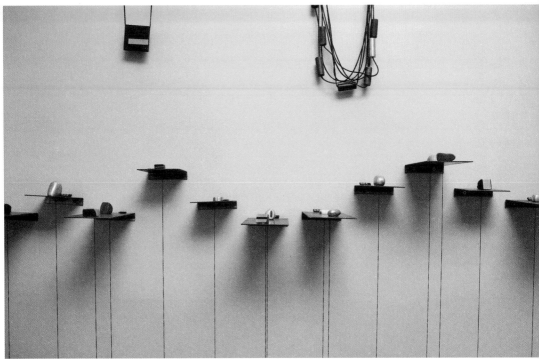

Ebano
27 rue Durantin, 75018 ☎ 01 42 51 71 29
www.ebano.fr
Open Tuesday–Sunday 2pm–6.30pm
Métro Abbesses, Blanche **Bus** 80, 95
The shop is not accessible for wheelchairs but most items can be brought to clients from the window display

This small jewellery shop specialises in very simple but sophisticated pieces made from natural materials such as ebony wood and aluminium. Even if you can't afford the simply beautiful wooden pendants or a solid silver ring, Senegalese-born Hamath Sall and his Italian wife Milana Pesce also make inexpensive but visually stunning pieces. Try on a bracelet made from their own metal and brightly coloured resin 'rocks', something to suit any occasion – from formal to funky.

Johanna Gullichsen, Textile Craft & Design

74 rue du Cherche Midi, 75006 ☎ 01 42 22 12 67
www.johannagullichsen.com
Open Tuesday–Saturday 11am–7pm
Métro Saint Placide, Vaneau, Rennes **Bus** 39, 70, 87, 89, 94, 96
The shop is not easily accessible for wheelchairs as the entrance is a bit high, but staff are happy to lend a helping hand when needed

The textile designs sold in this stylish shop are all the brainchild of Finnish designer Johanna Gullichsen. Her minimalist fabric is constructed from natural fibres and consists of simple, two-coloured stripes and neat broken lines. From dusky yellow canvas shoulder bags to duck-egg blue napkins and aprons, this is a great place to buy presents for amateur chefs or house-proud friends. The clean lines of these kitchen fabrics will bring a Scandinavian summer into any kitchen. Her distinctive cloth can also be bought by the yard for your own sewing projects.

Tamano

18 passage Moliere, 75003, between 157 rue Saint Martin and rue Quincampoix. You may need to knock loudly on the door as Tamano's workshop is at the rear of the shop ☎ 01 42 78 09 53
www.tamano-paris.com
Open Tuesday–Saturday 8.45am–6pm **Métro** Rambuteau, Étienne Marcel **Bus** 38, 39, 47
The workshop is accessible but there is very little room for a wheelchair

Kumihimo are knotted sandals, intricate fascinating artworks you can wear on your feet, and are the speciality of Japanese shoemaker Tamano Nagashima. Taught by a master shoemaker, she employs her patiently learnt skills to create tantalizing, silken wedding shoes and soft baby booties. In her small atelier she stitches custom-made footwear, from African wax-resist print espadrilles to two-tone brogues with bright green laces. Choose from over 120 colours and which leather or cord you want to adorn your feet, then let them be measured and a week later this master shoemaker will present you with a pair of quite unique, perfectly formed shoes. Tamano's designs can also be posted abroad if you are not staying in Paris for very long.

Écritoire

51 rue Saint-Martin, 75004 ☎ 01 42 78 01 18
www.ecritoire.fr **Open** Monday–Saturday 11am–7pm
Métro Hôtel de Ville, Châtelet, Rambuteau **Bus** 38, 47, 75
The shop is accessible for wheelchairs but it may be hard
to turn around

Écritoire translates as 'ink stand' and this friendly shop
dedicated to writing has the atmosphere of an old-fashioned
stationers but is stocked with inventive, modern designs. If
you need a new nib for your fountain pen or some pastel-
coloured circular envelopes, this is the ideal place. As well
as real feather quills, this is a good shop to pick up some
rather sophisticated presents made by French artisans.

La Tuile à Loup

35 rue Daubenton, 75005 ☎ 01 47 07 28 90
www.latuilealoup.com **Open** Monday 1pm–7pm, Tuesday–
Saturday 10.30am–7pm and by appointment at other
times **Métro** Censier Daubenton, Place Monge **Bus** 27, 47
There is disabled access to the shop

La Tuile à Loup (the Tile Wolf) may sound a bit daunting
but this is a welcoming shop, specialising in artisanal
ceramics, baskets and pewter kitchenware made in
France. The owner trawls the country looking for 'objets
des provinces', beautiful things made by craftspeople
keeping alive traditions specific to each region. It is hard
to enter this shop and not immediately feel very happy.

Izrael, L'Épicerie du Monde

30 rue François Miron, 75004 ☎ 01 42 72 66 23
Open Monday–Friday 9.30am–1pm and 2.30pm–7pm, Saturday 9am–7pm
Métro Hotel de Ville, Saint-Paul, Pont Marie **Bus** 69, 76, 96
There is disabled access to the shop

If you want to conjure up the banquets found in the tales of the Arabian Nights, this is the place to find more than 1001 delicious things to eat. The shop is like a compact oriental bazaar, full of baskets overflowing with visually enticing delicacies, including bright green pistachio nuts, dried figs tied together with raffia, sacks of pale couscous, crisp, sweet candied angelica and 25 different sorts of grinding pepper. This grocers sells an amazing array of food from the Middle and Far East, but you can also get French liqueurs such as the inimitable absinthe and even jars of British Marmite.

Bio C' Bon

9 place Pigalle, 75010 ☎ 01 49 95 03 43
www.bio-c-bon.eu **Open** Monday–Saturday 10am–8pm, Sunday
10am–1pm **Métro** Pigalle **Bus** 30, 54, 67, Monmartrobus
Only the ground floor is accessible for wheelchair users
but you can compile a shopping list from their website

In this modern organic grocers you'll find crisp white
fennel bulbs and tiny purple fronds of sprouted brassica
in traditional wooden crates. On the ground floor there's a
profusion of fresh vegetables and fruit, and upstairs there's
more in the way of storeroom cupboard essentials. This is
a great place to do a weekly shop – the shop assistants
are friendly and the till queues extremely short.

La Ferme Saint Hubert Fromagerie

36 rue Rochechouart, 75009 ☎ 01 45 53 15 77
www.la-ferme-saint-hubert-de-paris.com
Open Monday–Saturday 9am–9pm, closed Sunday
Métro Barbes Rochechouart, Anvers **Bus** 85
The shop is wheelchair accessible

This wonderful fromagerie is a cornucopia of French produce,
stocking nearly every cheese made in France – over 200 of them.
Amiable owners Paulette and Henry Voy are 'master cheese
tasters' and also stock regional cider, jams and saucissons. The
original shop fittings include traditional veined marble walls
and ornate mirrors – a beautiful place to stock up on le Bleu
crémeux de Haute Loire or Camembert 'artisanal au lait cru'.

Restaurants

Polidor

41 rue Monsieur-le-Prince, 75006 ☎ 01 43 26 95 34
www.polidor.com
Open every day 12pm–2.30pm and 7pm–12.30am, except Sunday
when the restaurant closes at 11pm
Métro Odéon, Cluny-La Sorbonne **RER** Luxembourg
Bus 21, 27, 38, 58, 84, 89
The restaurant is accessible for wheelchairs (there's a very small
step at the entrance), but does not have an adapted toilet

Since 1845 Polidor has been serving traditional French dishes
to discerning Parisians. This is a very sociable place to eat,
but like a few other long-established restaurants, no music is
played here, so both conversation and wine can flow without any
distractions. Perhaps, like the writers Rimbaud, Victor Hugo
and Hemingway you'll appreciate their down-to-earth main
courses and desserts.

Le Terroir Parisien

20 rue Saint Victor, 75005 ☎ 01 44 31 54 54
www.yannick-alleno.com/restaurant/paris-le-terroir-parisien/
Open daily from 'breakfast to dinner', including a few public holidays and most of August
Métro Maubert-Mutualité, Cardinal Lemoine **Bus** 24, 47, 63, 86, 87
The restaurant is wheelchair accessible, the toilet is not specially adapted but is on the ground floor

With its huge mirrors, wooden walls, uncluttered look and simple, beautifully designed furniture, it is a real pleasure to be seated at Yannick Alléno's latest culinary offspring. The semi-open kitchen suggests that diners are participating in an exciting venture – to appreciate outstanding cooking from a world-renowned chef. Alléno transformed the former Maison de la Mutualité into a stunning bistro, making Le Terroir Parisien a sophisticated place to enjoy superb dishes made mainly with ingredients from the Ile de France, the area surrounding Paris. Order the tasty potato, eel and leek soup, the roast lamb with baby vegetables followed by a poached pear drizzled with honey collected by Parisian bees.

Aquarius
40 rue de Gergovie, 75014 ☎ 01 45 41 36 88
Open Monday–Saturday 12pm–2.15pm and 7pm–11pm
Métro Plaisance, Pernety **Bus** 58, 62
The ground floor restaurant is accessible but does not have a specially adapted toilet

Entering this vegetarian restaurant is like going back in time thirty years. If you're feeling nostalgic, the hand-made wooden tables are inlaid with zodiac signs and even the menu is nicely old-fashioned. Even if you are not a fan of astrological designs, join the locals who come here for couscous or lasagne followed by cheesecake. There are very few vegan options here, however; mainly hummus and pita bread with salad.

Le Repaire de Cartouche

99 rue Amelot, 75011 ☎ 01 47 00 25 86
Open Monday–Saturday for lunch and dinner
(from about 12pm–11pm, with a lull around
3pm–5pm), closed during August
Métro Saint-Sebastien Froissart, Filles de
Calvaire **Bus** 20, 65, 96
The main room has access for wheelchairs
but not the upper floor

The dark wood-panelled rooms and white table
linen announce that Le Repaire de Cartouche
(named after a notorious highwayman figure)
is a traditional and well-established Parisian
restaurant. The confident 'cuisine de terroir'
menu offers an abundance of down-to-earth
classic French dishes. Typical hors d'oeuvres
include paté, followed by pan fried beef or
grilled fish. The wine list reveals the owner's
predilection for regional French grape
varieties, and complement the dishes well.

Le Gorille Blanc

4 impasse Guéménée, 75004 ☎ 01 42 72 08 45
www.legorilleblanc.fr

Open Monday–Saturday 12pm–2.30pm and 7.30pm–11pm, and on some bank holidays. It's a good idea to make a reservation **Métro** Bastille, Saint-Paul **Bus** 20, 29, 65, 69, 76

The ground floor restaurant is accessible but does not have a specially adapted toilet

Named after the rare albino gorilla in Marseille zoo, Le Gorille Blanc's speciality is French cuisine from the south-west of France. Bernard Areny and his son serve up inventive dishes accompanied by a good selection of regional wines. Tucked down a quiet side street, this is a good place to have a quiet lunch as music (mainly Chopin) is only played in the evenings. Carnivores will enjoy the regional ham salad with balsamic vinegar dressing and the braised rabbit with raisins and carrots. You might also want to try the delicious Pyrenees sheeps' cheese made by Belloc Abbey monks, usually served with black cherry jam.

Le Grand Appetit

9 rue de la Cerisaie, 75004 ☎ 01 40 27 04 95
Open Monday–Friday for lunch only (from around 12pm–3pm)
Métro Bastille **Bus** 20, 29, 65, 76, 86, 87, 91, 96
The restaurant is accessible but the small toilet isn't easy to negotiate

This old, stone-walled building has been home to this thriving macrobiotic restaurant for over 25 years. It has a very relaxed, almost familial atmosphere, and the old-fashioned decor adds to its nonchalant appeal. Queue up for a bowl of vegan delicacies, such as chickpeas with seaweed or millet and vegetables, followed by a subtly flavoured sugar- and dairy-free apricot pudding. You have to lay your own table, but this informal touch just makes diners feel at home. Help yourself to free herbal tea, and if you want to try cooking the dish you've just eaten, the owner also has a vegetarian wholefood shop next door.

La Laiterie Saint Clotilde

64 rue de Bellechasse, 75007 ☎ 01 45 51 74 61
Open weekdays around 12.30pm for lunch, 8pm to late
for dinner, closed in August **Métro** Varenne, Rue du Bac,
Solférino **Bus** 63, 68, 69, 84, 98
The restaurant is accessible but the toilet is not adapted

It was a bit of a surprise to find this friendly neighbourhood
restaurant in the middle of an area full of government
buildings. The decor could be described as 'modern retro',
with Formica chairs, red leatherette benches and a wine
list written in chalk on black painted walls. The concise
menu changes daily, so let yourself be pleasantly surprised
by whatever is on offer when you arrive.

La Ferrandaise

8 rue de Vaugirard, 75006 ☎ 01 43 26 36 36
www.laferrandaise.com **Open** Tuesday–Friday for lunch,
Monday–Saturday for dinner, until midnight on Friday and
Saturday, closed on Sunday and public holidays **Métro** Odéon,
Cluny-La Sorbonne **RER** Luxembourg **Bus** 58, 84, 89, 96
The restaurant is accessible but the toilet is not adapted

Fashionably close to both La Sorbonne and the Jardin du
Luxembourg, this traditional French restaurant is renowned
for its hearty stews and numerous beef dishes. Named
after the Ferrandaise breed of cow, the menu unashamedly
celebrates bovine delicacies. In addition, there is a fine
selection of cheeses and excellent regional wines.

Restaurant Da Lat

19 rue Louis Bonnet, 75011 ☎ 01 43 38 22 72
Open every day 11am to about 1.30am, including most bank holidays
Métro Belleville **Bus** 26, 46 (but neither are very close by)
The ground floor restaurant is accessible but the toilet is not adapted for wheelchairs

This restaurant is often filled with local Southeast Asian families but because Da Lat doesn't play piped music, it remains a convivial, relaxed place even on Sundays. Service is fast and efficient and the portions are generous. Try mixing dishes from different cuisines – start with Chinese dim sum prawn dumplings brought to you in a bamboo steamer, followed by a Vietnamese shredded green papaya salad with a sweet vinegar dressing. Then slurp your way through the best Beef Phô (noodle soup) outside Hanoi.

Restaurant in the Musée Dapper

5 bis rue Paul Valéry, 75116 ☎ 01 45 00 91 75 for the museum or 01 45 00 31 73 for restaurant reservations
www.dapper.fr

Open The museum is open Wednesday, Friday–Monday 11am–7pm, closed on Tuesday, Thursday and public holidays.
The restaurant is open Monday–Thursday 12pm–2.30pm
Métro Victor Hugo, Kleber **RER** Charles de Gaulle-Étoile **Bus** 30, 32, 52, 82
There is access for wheelchair users to the restaurant and museum

The Musée Dapper is a fascinating museum of African, Caribbean and Diasporic cultures. Named after a Dutch humanist from the 17th century, the permanent collection includes mainly historic artefacts while temporary exhibitions focus more on contemporary artworks, photography and video projections. The stylish restaurant is located in the basement and serves excellent lunches. Try their courgette carpaccio with smoked salmon and the capitaine fish with spicy 'diable' sauce or a vegetable couscous. Afterwards, you can browse the small museum bookshop, also in the dining room.

Restaurant de La Maison de l'Amerique Latine

217 boulevard St Germain, 75007 ☎ 01 49 54 75 00
www.mal217.org
Open Monday–Friday for lunch only, closed on public holidays, from 21 December–1 January and around
21 July–20 August **Métro** Solférino, Rue du Bac **RER** Musée d'Orsay, Aérogare Invalides **Bus** 63, 68, 69, 83, 84, 94
The ground floor restaurant is accessible but does not have a specially adapted toilet

It is often hard to get access to private gardens in Paris but dining here gives you the opportunity to enjoy one of the
loveliest views in the capital. On fine summer days you can enjoy world class cuisine on the outdoor terrace overlooking
an expansive lawn surrounded by tall trees. Even in winter, sitting in elegant 18th-century rooms hung with chandeliers
make this a very civilised place to appreciate fine wines and exquisite food. Although their cuisine is traditionally French
it also has Italian influences, such as their mullet with dill, tomatoes and leafy green mizuma followed by a pear and
chocolate tiramisu.

Le Hangar

12 impasse Berthaud, 75003 ☎ 01 42 74 55 41
Open Tuesday–Saturday 12pm–2.30pm and 7.30pm–11pm,
closed in August **Métro** Rambuteau **Bus** 29, 38, 47, 75
The restaurant is wheelchair accessible but has a small
toilet door

After enduring the noise and crowds of the nearby
Pompidou Centre, this is a calm spot to have lunch or
dinner. Located in a quiet cul-de-sac next to the Anne Frank
garden, Le Hangar is the ideal place to appreciate traditional
French cooking. In summer sit on the small outdoor terrace
to savour a bowl of delicious pumpkin and chestnut soup
followed by grilled sea bream with mashed potatoes.

Montécao

17–19 rue Saint-Paul, 75004 ☎ 01 42 71 06 07
www.levillagesaintpaul.com
Open Wednesday–Friday 9.30am–9.45pm, Monday and
Sunday 9.30am–8.30pm, closed Tuesday
Métro Saint-Paul, Pont Marie **Bus** 67, 69, 76, 96
The restaurant is wheelchair accessible

Khalida Bourahla runs this unpretentious restaurant in the
pretty village Saint Paul. The tranquil courtyard feels like
a southern European piazza, making this the perfect place
to enjoy Mediterranean food. Inside, there's a glass-roofed
terrace to sip sweet mint tea in the afternoon. After dusk,
linger to dine in the quiet square in front of the restaurant.

Cafés

A Priori Thé

35-7 Galerie Vivienne, rue des Petit Champs, 75002
☎ 01 42 97 48 75
www.apriorithe.com
Open Monday–Friday 9am–6pm, Saturday 9am–6.30pm, Sunday brunch 12pm–4pm, high tea 4pm–6.30pm. Open on public holidays except for Christmas Day and New Year's Day
Métro Bourse, Pyramides **Bus** 20, 29, 38, 48
The café is wheelchair accessible, but enter Galerie Vivienne via rue de la Banque. The toilet is rather small for wheelchair users

Galerie Vivienne is one of the prettiest shopping arcades in Paris and even on wet days, it's a pleasure to wander through this 19th-century glass-roofed passage. After some smart window shopping, enjoy a cup of A Priori Thé's delicious herbal tea sitting under their capacious parasols. The lunches here are also very good, with a few cooked vegetarian meals at lunchtime as well as cheesecake or scones for tea. Music is sometimes played indoors, but not in the external passage.

Le Bal

6 impasse de la Défense, 75018 ☎ 01 44 70 75 51
www.le-bal.fr
Open Wednesday–Friday 12pm–2.30pm, Saturday 11am–3pm, Wednesday–Saturday 8pm–10.30pm,
Sunday 11am–4pm (the bookshop and exhibition spaces are open at other times, see the website for details)
Métro Place de Clichy, Fourche **Bus** 54, 68, 74, 80, 81, 95
Le Bal is wheelchair accessible

Le Bal café is a reason to celebrate being in Paris – not only does this publicly funded art centre have a large gallery in the basement, it also has a well-stocked bookshop and welcoming café. The food is superb – from an incredibly smooth lunchtime cauliflower soup to the perfectly cooked fish and baby carrots in the evening. The two women chefs certainly know their way round sophisticated French cooking but they are still happy to offer a hearty brunch on Sunday for laid-back locals – and anyone else dropping by. Try their freshly baked scones or a tarte aux pommes with crème fraiche after a plate of hot kippers. The coffee is also great here, whatever time of day.

Le Petit Saint Paul

40 rue Saint Paul, 75004
Open Tuesday–Sunday 7am–9.30pm, closed on Monday and for two weeks over Christmas, two weeks in August and from 1–8 May
Métro Saint-Paul, Sully-Morland **Bus** 67, 69, 76
The café is accessible but does not have a specially adapted toilet

This unassuming café on the edge of the village Saint Paul is a good place to drop in and have a chat with the locals. For lunch, enjoy a steak accompanied by a glass of Burgundy and French fries or, if you are just looking for a snack, order a croque monsieur. This unpretentious bistro won't be too expensive and is just off the tourist route, so you'll usually get a place to sit.

Balbuzard

54 rue Rene Boulanger, 75010 ☎ 01 42 08 60 20
www.lebalbuzard.com **Open** Monday–Saturday
12pm–2.30pm and 7pm–1am **Métro** République, Jaques
Bonsergent, Temple **Bus** 20, 56, 65, 75
There is no access for wheelchairs to the upstairs toilet
but the ground floor is accessible

Balbuzard café has an affable, laid-back atmosphere.
The glass mirrors behind the bar are reminiscent of Manet's
painting of the Folies Bergère, but this small brasserie feels
homely rather than theatrical. This is a good place to try
Corsican wines and dishes from the region. The menu is not
that extensive, but portions are huge and the food delicious.

A L'Heure du Thé

23 rue Lacépède, 75005 ☎ 01 47 07 60 52
Open Tuesday–Saturday 11am–7.30pm, Sunday 11am–6pm,
closed on public holidays **Métro** Place Monge **Bus** 47
The shop and café are accessible

The title of this refined salon could translate as 'time for
tea', and with over 100 loose teas in black enamel caddies,
it's obvious where the patron's speciality lies. The names
of the teas are beguiling, and if you are tempted, order a
pot of lapsang souchong or a Japanese green gyoukuro in
the tea room at the rear. Non-tea drinkers are also well
catered for, from bottles of velvety smooth carrot juice to
salad with quiche for a substantial lunch.

L'Estaminet des Enfants Rouges

39 rue de Bretagne, 75003
☎ 01 42 72 28 12
www.lestaminetdesenfantsrouges.com
Open Tuesday–Saturday 9am–8pm, Sunday 9am–3pm, closed Monday
Métro Arts et Métiers, Temple, Filles du Calvaire **Bus** 20, 75
The café is wheelchair accessible but does not have a specially adapted toilet

L'Estaminet means 'the Tavern', but this small café is more like a rustic, laid-back bistro than a place for tankards and beer songs. The owner is an enterprising chef who creates an inventive menu using mainly organic produce from independent farms and her menu changes daily. L'Estaminet is also an ideal place for a relaxed Sunday brunch overlooking the bustling Marché des Enfants Rouges.

Mamie Gâteux

66 rue du Cherche Midi, 75006 ☎ 01 42 22 32 15
www.mamie-gateaux.com
Open Monday–Friday 11.30am–2.30pm, Sunday to 3pm, closed from around 23 July–23 August
Métro Rennes, Vaneau, Saint-Placide **Bus** 39, 68, 70, 87, 89, 94, 95, 96
The café is wheelchair accessible but there is a small step at the entrance and a rather small toilet

This lovely old-fashioned tea room is a light-filled space to enjoy some excellent home cooking. The owner's Japanese wife creates unusual cakes and pastries, including cherry and pistachio tart, served through a small hatch in her tiny kitchen. She also bakes tasty, filling dishes for lunch, including a savoury vegetable crumble with parmesan and pine nuts as well as offering a few leafy salads on the menu. The decor is nostalgic, with dolls-house kitchens and blue ceramic flour canisters on wooden shelves. The red and white chequered paper mats on the tables add to the simple look and if you're tempted by anything on display, nip into the owner's recently opened brocante next door which sells bonbons and home-made biscuits and grandma-inspired bric-a-brac.

La Cortigiana Restaurant at Le Musée Maillol

59–61 rue de Grenelle, 75007 ☎ 01 42 22 59 58
www.museemaillol.com

Open every day 10.30am–7pm, open until 9.30pm on Friday, closed 25 December and 1 January (open on other bank holidays but closes early on 24 and 31 December)
Métro Rue du Bac, Sèvres-Babylone **Bus** 63, 68, 69, 83, 84, 94
The restaurant and museum are accessible for wheelchair users

Enjoy an Italian-inspired meal in the ancient vaulted cellar of this small Left Bank museum. After wandering round the Aristide Maillol sculptures and the temporary exhibitions upstairs, this is a nice place to have lunch with friends. Look forward to a buffalo mozarella and pomodori tomato salad with a glass of chilled white wine after spending an hour or two looking at classical paintings. La Cortigiana is also an excellent place to enjoy a cup of afternoon tea with home-baked pastries.

Crêperie le Vieux Journal

17 rue Bréa, 75006 ☎ 01 43 26 90 49
Open every day 12pm–2pm and 6pm–10pm, closed 31 December and 1 January
Métro Vavin, Notre Dame des Champs **Bus** 58, 68, 82, 91
There is access for wheelchairs but the toilet is small

This friendly crêperie has been serving up cheap, filling meals for local students and passers-by for over 20 years. The formula is simple – serve tasty buckwheat pancakes with spinach, egg, cheese or ham fillings, pour out a few glasses of artisanal cider and the conversation will flow. The yellowing varnish covering the old newspapers pasted to the walls just adds to the charm of this unpretentious bistro.

The Tea Caddy

14 rue Saint Julien le Pauvre, 75005 ☎ 01 43 54 15 56
Open Saturday-Wednesday 11am–7pm, Thursday and Friday
11am–11pm **Métro** Saint Michel, Cluny-La Sorbonne, Maubert-
Mutualité **RER** Saint Michel **Bus** 21, 24, 27, 63, 85, 86, 87
The tea room is accessible but there is no adapted toilet

Many Parisian cafés serve real tea in teapots, but not
many have such a wide range of blends as the Tea Caddy.
Having opened in 1928, this is a well-known Parisian
institution, and entering the wood-panelled dining room
feels like walking back in time. This is one of the few
places to enjoy a traditional British high tea, with
Devon clotted cream and homemade scones.

Le Dit Vin

68 rue Blanche, 75009 ☎ 01 45 26 27 37
Open Monday–Friday 12pm–3pm and 6.30pm–9.30pm,
Saturday 11am–1.30pm and 6.30pm–9.30pm
Métro Blanche, Liège, Place de Clichy **Bus** 68, 74
The tables are accessible, but the toilets are not

Le Dit Vin means 'the speaking wine' and this small bistro
is basically a convivial room for wine tasting where the
chef just happens to enjoy conjuring up some interesting
dishes. Choose a wine from the many bottles on the open
shelves, then sample a variety of dishes from the buffet.
If you can manage it, ask for a slice of tarte aux mirabelles
(little plums) to end your gourmet lunch.

Bookshops

Musée d'Art Brut and Art Singulier – Halle Saint Pierre Museum of Naive Art Bookshop

Halle Saint Pierre, 2 rue Ronsard, 75018 ☎ 01 42 58 72 89
www.hallesaintpierre.org
Open Monday–Friday 10am–6pm, Saturday 10am–7pm, Sunday 11am–6pm, during August the museum is open weekdays 12pm–6pm only, closed at weekends. Closed 25 December, 1 January, 1 May, 14 July and 15 August
Métro Barbès Rochechouart, Château Rouge, Abbesses
Bus 30, 54 and the Montmartrobus
The bookshop is accessible but not the upper floor of the museum

This large industrial-looking building at the foot of the Butte Montmartre is often overlooked by visitors to the city, yet this museum hosts some of the most intriguing exhibitions in Paris. The Halles Saint Pierre specialises in showing work by internationally renowned artists who have no formal art training yet produce strangely compelling paintings, textiles and sculptures. As well as the fascinating temporary displays of 'art brut', there is a well-stocked bookshop which sells posters, catalogues, and other publications about outsider art.

L'Aigle Ignore

23 rue Condorcet, 75009
Open Monday–Saturday 12pm–2pm and 4pm–7pm
Métro Poissonière, Anvers **Bus** 26, 42, 43, 85
The shop is on the ground floor but has a small step at the entrance and is very crowded with books

The 'Ignored Eagle' second-hand bookshop is a great place to browse. French language titles are piled high on old wooden bookshelves and there is no cataloguing system, so whatever is there one day might be gone the next. The shop never plays music and the owner doesn't even have a phone. *'Pas de bruit'* ('no noise at all'), he replied when asked if his shop was always as quiet. You might be lucky and find an exquisite leatherbound *Dictionary of Herbs* printed in 1764 or pick up a novel by Alphonse Daudet – one of many paperbacks for only a couple of euros in a box by the front door.

ɦakespeare and Co

rue de la Bûcherie, 75005 ☎ 01 43 25 40 93

ᴇn Monday–Friday 10am–11pm, Saturday and Sunday 11am–11pm

tro Saint Michel **RER** Saint Michel Notre Dame **Bus** 21, 27, 24, 38, 47, 63, 85, 86, 87

ere is a step into the building and stairs to the upper floor

th its illustrious history (when he couldn't find anyone to print his book *Ulysses*, James Joyce was discovered and
st published by the former owner), this rather ramshackle bookshop remains a bibliophile's delight. The tables are
ᴇd high with an idiosyncratic assortment of English language books, from American novels to thin volumes of poetry
m as yet unknown writers. The main bookshop plays French chansons and can get crowded, but the antiquarian
partment to the left remains a haven of peace and quiet.

Florence Loewy ... by Artists

9 rue de Thorigny, 75003 ☎ 01 44 78 98 45
www.florenceloewy.com
Open Tuesday–Saturday 2pm–7pm, closed on public holidays
Métro Filles de Calvaire, Saint-Sébastien Froissart, Chemin Vert **Bus** 20, 29, 65, 96
There is wheelchair access to the bookshop and gallery

Unusual wooden bookshelves with curved edges fill the main space in this small bookshop near to the Picasso Museum. Artists' books such as David Shrigley's *Worried* and American artist Lawrence Wiener's more conceptual publications can be found here in abundance. To the right of the main room there is a more intimate gallery devoted to showing work by international artists. This grey-walled room is an exceptionally restful, quiet space and even if you can't afford the photographs or drawings on display, you can always buy a copy of the artist's limited-edition book from the knowledgeable staff who work here.

Maison d'Europe et d'Orient – Centre Culturel Européen

3 passage Hennel, 75012 ☎ 01 40 24 00 55
www.sildav.org **Open** Monday–Friday 10am–1pm and
2pm–7pm, closed on public holidays
Métro Gare de Lyon, Reuilly-Diderot **Bus** 26, 29, 57
There is disabled access to the bookshop

This small but inviting centre for European culture tries to
bridge gaps between the West and Eastern Europe. They
also publish books on theatre and the arts, under the name
Éditions l'Espace d'un Instant, focusing on drama and writing
from the Balkans. Children's bilingual picture books can also
be found here, including stories in both French and Arabic.

Librairie Gourmande

92–6 rue Montmartre, 75002 ☎ 01 43 54 47 27
www.librairiegourmande.fr **Open** Monday–Saturday
11am–7pm, closed on Sunday and public holidays
Métro Bourse, Etienne Marcel, Montorgueil-Sentier,
Grands Boulevards **Bus** 67, 74, 85
Only the ground floor is accessible for wheelchairs

From the street, this bookshop looks rather unassuming
and nondescript. Once inside, however, it is so full of books
on food and cooking that it is hard to know where to begin.
There are tomes by renowned French chefs, cookery books
for children, illustrated guides to help you bake macaroons
and even anthologies of rare, heirloom vegetables.

La Librairie des Editeurs Associés

10 rue Tournefort, 75005 ☎ 01 43 36 81 19
www.lesediteursassocies.com **Open** Wednesday–Saturday
2pm–6pm, closed on public holidays **Métro** Place Monge,
Cardinal Lemoine **Bus** 27, 47, 84, 89
The bookshop is accessible for wheelchair users

It doesn't have the most inspiring name but the Bookshop of
Associated Editors does have a wonderful selection of both
fiction and non-fiction titles. This showcase for independent
French language publishers has many titles you won't
find anywhere else. Every shelf is full of surprises; from
limited-edition, beautifully illustrated fairy tales to grown-up
treatises on history and politics – this is a shop to treasure.

La Librairie Galerie Emmanuel Perrotin

76 rue de Turenne, 75003 ☎ 01 42 16 79 79
www.perrotin.com **Open** Tuesday–Saturday 11am–7pm,
closed in August and on public holidays
Métro Saint-Sébastien Froissart **Bus** 20, 65, 96
There is no disabled access to this bookshop

Located in the large courtyard in front of the eye-catching
Galerie Perrotin, this small, specialist bookshop has some
fascinating books and magazines on fine art in stock, many
of which accompany the exhibitions in the internationally-
renowned art space next door. This is also one of the few
bookshops where you can buy *The Drawer*, a magazine,
as the title suggests, all about contemporary drawing.

Librairie Le Phénix

72 boulevard de Sébastopol, 75003 ☎ 01 42 72 70 31
www.librairielephenix.fr
Open Monday–Saturday 10am–7pm, closed on public holidays
Métro Réaumur-Sébastopol **Bus** 20, 29, 38, 39, 47
The ground floor is accessible but not the basement or 1st floor

This distinctive bookshop specialises in Chinese literature and books about travel and culture in the Far East.
It is not only one of the few places in Paris to buy a Chinese language newspaper, they also stock Thai and
Vietnamese books as well as maps and French non-fiction about the region. In front of the upstairs window
you'll also find hogs hair brushes, Chinese ink and books in English on the art of calligraphy. This is also an
excellent place to buy paper cuts, hand-painted scrolls and beautiful greeting cards.

Lettres et Images

58 Galerie Vivienne, 4 rue des Petits-Champs, 75002 ☎ 01 42 86 88 18
www.galerie-vivienne.com
Open Tuesday–Friday 10.45am–2pm and 3pm–7pm, Saturday 1pm–7pm, closed on public holidays
Métro Bourse, Quatre-Septembre, Pyramides **Bus** 20, 29, 39, 74, 85
The shop is wheelchair accessible, but be sure to enter the Galerie Vivienne via the rue de la Banque as this entrance
offers step-free access

Entering Catherine Aubrey's small bookshop is like being invited into a comfortable living room full of thoughtful,
illustrated books. She doesn't just stock French language poetry from independent presses; dark monochrome etching
hang in the window, turning the front of this diminutive shop into a compact gallery space. The owner will spend time
discussing the merits of each purchase, making this bookshop the epitome of 'slow shopping'. She has a few collection
of poetry in English, but the large collection of books and original prints is mainly of work by French writers and artists.

Librairie Galignani

224 rue de Rivoli, 75001 ☎ 01 42 60 76 07
www.galignani.com **Open** Monday–Saturday 10am–7pm,
closed on public holidays **Métro** Tuileries **Bus** 68, 72
The ground floor is wheelchair accessible but there is no
access to the mezzanine

Renowned for being the first English language bookshop
on the continent, Galignani is still one of the most
important 'librairies' in Paris, where elegant, knowledgeable
customers can be seen browsing richly illustrated art books
and literary masterpieces. The handsome wooden shelves
are weighed down with mainly English books but there are
also sections devoted to French publications.

Ofr. Bookshop, Librairie, HQ

20 rue Dupetit-Thouars, 75003 ☎ 01 42 45 72 88
www.ofrsystem.com **Open** Monday–Saturday 10am–8pm,
Sunday 2pm–7pm **Métro** Temple, République, Filles du Calvaire
Access for wheelchairs is difficult

Ofr. is much more than an art and design bookshop.
Next to piles of very fashionable magazines, customers
can try on distinctive bamboo framed sunglasses or
brightly coloured deck shoes. As well as an emphasis on
intelligent graphic design, photography and 20th-century
textiles, there are also numerous artist monographs. At
the rear is an exhibition space which might show anything
from pencil drawings to all-encompassing installations.

La Chambre Claire

14 rue Saint-Sulpice, 75006 ☎ 01 46 34 04 31 for the photography bookshop, 01 43 59 17 71 for the cinema bookshop
www.la-chambre-claire.fr
Open Tuesday–Saturday 11am–7pm, closed on public holidays
Métro Odéon, Mabillon, Saint-Sulpice, Saint Germain des Prés, Cluny-La Sorbonne
Bus 58, 63, 70, 84, 86, 87, 89, 96
There are two steps at the entrance

La Chambre Claire is one of the best specialist photography bookshops in Europe, and this is a great place to browse
if you are interested in either recent or 20th-century images from around the world. In addition to the many monographs
and exhibition catalogues you can also pick up a magazine or two, including the wistful *Edwarda*. As there are two
bookshops in this old building, you might want to venture downstairs to Librarie Contact to find books on the cinema
or just make a fleeting visit to appreciate the atmospheric old stone walls.

Attica: La Librairie des Langues

96 boulevard Richard Lenoir, 75011 ☎ 01 55 28 80 14
www.attica.fr
Open Monday–Saturday 10am–7pm, closed on public
holidays
Métro Oberkampf, Parmentier **Bus** 46, 56, 96
The shop is wheelchair accessible

This spacious bookshop is renowned for the thousands of
books and films it stocks in many different languages. If
you are looking for bilingual children's books in Spanish
and English, a Teach Yourself Swahili language course,
DVDs of plays by Shakespeare, a guide to Italian cinema
or Japanese nursery songs, this is the perfect location.

WH Smith

248 rue de Rivoli, 75001 ☎ 01 44 77 88 99
www.whsmith.fr **Open** Monday–Saturday 9am–7pm,
Sunday, bank holidays 12.30pm–7pm, closed 1 January, 25
December, 1 May **Métro** Concorde, Tuileries **Bus** 24, 72
The shop is only accessible on the ground floor but
friendly staff will find books on other floors

Since 1903 WH Smith has been the largest English
language bookshop in Paris and the capacious interior
accommodates a wide range of magazines, newspapers,
literary and non-fiction titles. The building used to be a
tea shop and the atmosphere is still rather cosy, with
traditional wooden bookshelves filling every corner.

Galleries

Galerie Magda Danysz

78 rue Amelot, 75011 ☎ 01 45 83 38 51
Open Tuesday–Friday 11am–7pm, Saturday 2pm–7pm,
closed on public holidays
Métro Saint-Sébastien Froissart, Bréguet-Sabin
Bus 20, 29, 69, 96
There is access to the ground floor but not the first floor

The director of this small gallery in the 11th arrondissement
is very alert to what is current in the art world and often shows
new work from outside Europe. There is an emphasis on
Chinese artists as they have a sister gallery in Shanghai, but
Magda Danysz's selections are resolutely eclectic and well
informed. One of the gallery highlights is the subtle landscape
photography by Lang Yonliang, who uses 21st-century technology
to mimic delicate Chinese watercolour paintings. If you are
curious to see huge, playful interpretations of Leonardo's *Mona
Lisa*, you'll enjoy Gael Davrinche's irreverent, gestural paintings.

Galerie Michel Rein

42 rue de Turenne, 75003 ☎ 01 42 72 68 13
www.michelrein.com
Open Tuesday–Saturday 11am–7 pm, closed on public holidays
Métro Chemin Vert, Saint Paul **Bus** 29, 96
The gallery is not accessible to wheelchair users

Some of the world's most interesting artists show their work in this high-ceilinged, light-filled gallery. The Canadian photographer Allan Sekula reminds us of the ubiquity of manual labour in his solemn yet compelling photographs of working people. Elsewhere, Jimmie Durham's dense constellations of everyday objects and tender yet furious graphite drawings, demonstrate that this is a gallery replete with visual ideas. Raphaël Zarka makes abstract, solid oak sculptures (pictured) – huge, three-dimensional versions of his small, colourful ink drawings.

gnes B Galerie du Jour

4 rue Quincampoix, 75004 ☎ 01 44 54 55 90
www.galeriedujour.com **Open** Monday–Friday 10am–8pm,
losed on public holidays **Métro** Rambuteau, Châtelet les
alles **Bus** 29, 38, 47, 75
he gallery (and annex at rue Dieu) is accessible

he French fashion designer Agnes B not only has a very
uccessful chain of stylish boutiques, she also supports
ne visual arts with her much admired Galerie du Jour.
he small art bookshop at the entrance plays music but
he gallery behind is spacious and tranquil. There is an
mphasis on showing photographic work and this is a
reat place to see exciting, unusual exhibitions.

Galerie Dix9

19 rue des Filles de Calvaire, 75003 ☎ 01 42 78 91 77
www.galeriedix9.com **Open** Tuesday–Friday 2pm–7pm
and by appointment, closed in July, August and public
holidays **Métro** Filles de Calvaire **Bus** 9, 20, 65
The gallery is accessible to wheelchair users

A few years ago, this former car showroom was
transformed into a small, independent gallery showing
mainly work by French art school graduates. Hélène
Lacharmoise invites up-and-coming artists to exhibit here,
especially those who work across different disciplines.
Recent shows have included work by Mehdi-Georges Lahlou
(pictured) as well as Australian video-maker Tracey Moffat.

Les Ateliers de Paris

30 rue du Faubourg Saint Antoine, 75012 ☎ 01 44 73 83 50
www.ateliersdeparis.com **Open** Tuesday–Friday 10am–
1pm and 2pm–7pm, Saturday 1pm–7pm, closed on public
holidays and in August **Métro** Bastille **Bus** 76, 86, 87
There is access for wheelchairs in the gallery

Amongst the rather predictable brand name shops
on this main street is an inviting gallery where young
designers are invited to show their latest creations.
Many of the artisans have workshops tucked out of sight
behind the gallery and this enterprising space acts as
an 'incubator' for new talent. Expect to see innovative
garments, fashion accessories and ceramics.

Kadist Art Foundation

19 bis / 21 rue des Trois Frères, 75018 ☎ 01 42 51 83 49
www.kadist.org
Open Thursday–Sunday 2pm–7pm or by appointment
Métro Abbesses, Anvers **Bus** 30, 54, Montmartrobus
There is a step at the entrance, but the gallery and
meeting room are both on the ground floor

Located in an unprepossessing street in the 18th
arrondissement, this private art foundation organises some
outstanding shows of art that reflect on current ideas
about what it means to be a social being in an increasingly
fragmented society. There will always be something thought
provoking and intelligent to see in this innovative art space.

Galerie Camera Obscura

268 boulevard Raspail, 75014 ☎ 01 45 45 67 08
www.galeriecameraobscura.fr
Open Tuesday–Saturday 1pm–7pm, closed on public holidays
Métro Raspail, Denfert-Rochereau
There is access to the ground floor but not the basement gallery space

Near to the Parisian Observatory, this specialist photography gallery offers less evanescent (and perhaps more enigmatic) views than the night sky through a telescope. As delicate as pencil drawings, Yamamoto Masao's zen-like images have the pensive brevity of Haiku poetry. In one, a finger touches the surface of a pond above the silhouette of a small, feather-finned fish whilst in a night shot, lines of star-shaped firework lights are obscured by the dense black branches of a pine tree. This cool, air-conditioned gallery is a sophisticated place to view some remarkable work by international photographers.

Catherine Putman: Works on Paper

40 rue Quincampoix, 75004 ☎ 01 45 55 23 06
www.catherineputman.com
Open Tuesday–Saturday 2pm–7pm, closed on public holidays and from last week in July to end of August
Métro Châtelet-Les Halles, Rambuteau **Bus** 29, 38, 47
There is no access for wheelchairs to the gallery

This tranquil gallery on the first floor of a typically Parisian old building specialises in showing artworks on paper. Whether these are drawn, etched, torn or painted, this is the best gallery in Paris to see contemporary artworks using this medium of support. Bernard Moninot's 'Silent Listen' exhibition (pictured) was especially apt, and his exceptionally gentle graphite drawings capture the ineluctable silence of mortality. Don't be deterred by having to ring a doorbell and climb the stairs to gain entry – these white-walled rooms have much to offer.

Collection Galerie, Ateliers d'Art de France

rue Thorigny, 75003 ☎ 01 42 78 67 74

ww.ateliersdart.com/galerie-collection,9.htm

pen Tuesday–Saturday 11am–1pm and 2pm–7pm, closed on public holidays

létro Saint Paul, Arts et Métiers **Bus** 29, 75, 96

here is good access for wheelchair users

he Ateliers d'Art is the organisation responsible for supporting and promoting the work of French craftspeople,
federation of over 5,400 professionals. Their spacious, serene gallery shows group and one person exhibitions of
oth French and international artists and makers. You might see some perfectly executed ceramics which combine
raditional skills with a post-modern sensibility, or some surreal domestic objects such as a tattooed chair. In addition
o thematic shows, the curators organise conferences and debates on the applied arts. This is an excellent place to see
nnovative work in an exceptionally quiet, welcoming space.

Cultural centres

Institut Suédois à Paris

11 rue Payenne, 75003 ☎ 01 44 78 80 20
Free except for performances and special events
www.ccs.si.se
Open Tuesday–Sunday 12pm–6pm except during public holidays
Métro Saint-Paul, Chemin Vert, Filles de Calvaire **Bus** 29, 96
The exhibition space and café are accessible for wheelchair
users but the basement toilets are located down a flight of stairs

The Swedish Cultural Centre surrounds one of the nicest
courtyards in Le Marais, housed in the charming Hôtel de Marle
which dates from the 1560s. To the right of the entrance is a
compact exhibition space which mainly shows work by Swedish
artists and writers. On the left is a simple, unostentatious café
serving Swedish-inspired lunches but this sadly plays loud music.
In summer the courtyard is filled with white painted tables and
chairs so take your smoked salmon and herb sandwich outdoors,
well out of earshot of the music player. Many interesting events
are held here throughout the year, from culinary evenings to
literary encounters with Swedish authors. The centre describes
itself as offering a Franco-Swedish platform for cultural and
scientific meetings but anyone interested in Scandinavian culture
is welcome to attend and participate in discussions.

Centre Culturel Canadienne

5 rue de Constantine, 75007 ☎ 01 44 43 29 00
Free www.canadainternational.gc.ca/france
Open Monday–Thursday 10am–6pm, Thursday to 7pm,
closed Saturday, Sunday and most public holidays
Métro Invalides **RER** Invalides **Bus** 28, 49, 63, 69, 83
There is excellent disabled access throughout the building

This often overlooked cultural centre has a very inviting
first floor exhibition space where stimulating exhibitions
of Canadian art are shown. Twice a year, elegant 18th-
century rooms are filled with two- and three-dimensional
images by contemporary artists who work in a variety of
different media.

Collège des Bernardins

24 rue de Poissy, 75005 ☎ 01 53 10 74 44
Free www.collegedesbernardins.fr **Open** Monday–
Saturday 10am–6pm, Sunday 2pm–6pm, closed in August
Métro Cardinal Lemoine, Maubert-Mutualité
Bus 47, 63, 67, 86, 87, 89
The college, but not the ancient sacristy, is accessible

This theological college is more a religious than cultural
centre, but the transformation of the ancient sacristy into
a space to show contemporary art suggests an inclusive
agenda which exceeds mainstream Christian contemplation
and debate. The main hallway is a welcoming space with a
glass-walled bookshop and plenty of seating for tired legs.

Maison du Danemark

142 l'avenue Champs-Elysées, 75008 ☎ 01 56 59 17 40 or 01 56 59 17 44 for the Espace Culturel
Free www.maisondudanemark.dk **Open** Tuesday–Friday 1pm–7pm, Saturday, Sunday and most public holidays (during exhibitions) 1pm–6pm **Métro** Charles de Gaulles-Étoile **Bus** 22, 30, 31, 42, 52, 73, 92, 341 and the Balabus
There is good access for wheelchair users to the second floor gallery

Instead of following the crowds to the Arc de Triomphe, slip into the sophisticated Scandinavian interior of this little-known 'Espace Culturel'. Throughout the year, art exhibitions, talks, film screenings and even fashion shows are held in the Danish House which was built just after the Second World War. Displays have included the intelligent, enchanting work of Peter Callesen, a young Danish artist whose oeuvre consists of sculptures, each one made entirely from a single piece of intricately cut paper (pictured here). Sadly, the restaurant on the floor below plays piped music. If you prefer a more contemplative space, there is a small protestant church behind the Maison du Danemark, also built in the 1950s for members of the Danish community in Paris.

La Fondation Calouste Gulbenkian

39 boulevard de La Tour-Maubourg, 75007 ☎ 01 53 85 93 93
Free www.gulbenkian-paris.org **Open** Monday–Friday 9am–6pm, library open Monday, Wednesday,
Friday 10am–5pm, Tuesday and Thursday 10am–6pm, from 15 July–31 August by appointment only
Métro La Tour Maubourg, Varenne, Invalides **RER** Invalides **Bus** 28, 69
There is excellent access for wheelchair users throughout the building

The wealthy Armenian Calouste Gulbenkian acquired a huge art collection in Paris in the first half of the 20th century
and bequeathed his vast fortune to the Portuguese foundation named after him. Today its philanthropic and educational
activities extend to bringing Portuguese culture to the French capital in this serene building. The first floor galleries tend to
focus on showing work by Portuguese artists and recent exhibitions have included the compelling, psychologically intense
pastel drawings by Paula Rego and the black and white documentary prints of French-Portuguese photographer Gérard
Castello-Lopes. The library is also an excellent resource for anyone studying lusophone culture, from Lisbon poets to Latin
American novelists. With over 90,000 volumes this is the largest Portuguese language library outside Brazil and Portugal.

Centre Culturel Suisse

38 rue des Francs-Bourgeois, 75003 ☎ 01 42 71 44 50 **Free** except for special events such as talks and concerts
www.ccsparis.com **Open** Tuesday–Sunday 1pm–7pm, closed public holidays. The bookshop at 32 rue des Francs-
Bourgeois is open Tuesday–Thursday 10am–6pm, Saturday, Sunday and public holidays 1pm–7pm
Métro Hôtel de Ville, Rambuteau, Saint Paul, Chemin Vert **Bus** 29, 75
There is wheelchair access to the bookshop but not the first floor galleries

Picturesque Le Marais is the area to establish a cultural centre in Paris, the city that seems to have more foreign institutes
than any other worldwide. Plenty of beautiful old mansions have been converted into exhibition spaces, including the sedate
yet modern Swiss Cultural Centre. Although the architecturally interesting building is in the middle of the fashionable rue
des Francs-Bourgeois, the interior is surprisingly calm and tranquil. Group exhibitions of contemporary art by mainly Swiss
artists are held here as well as dance performances and conferences. The ground floor bookshop is a mecca for serious art
lovers as well as anyone wanting to pick up monographs on artists Pippilotti Rist or Thomas Hirschhorn. One publication
reminds us that Giacometti, Rousseau and Le Corbusier, who all lived and worked in France, were actually Swiss citizens.

Places to stay

Le Pavillon de la Reine

28 place des Vosges, 75003 ☎ 01 40 29 19 19
www.pavillon-de-la-reine.com
Métro Saint-Paul, Chemin Vert, Bastille **Bus** 20, 29, 65, 69, 76, 96
The hotel is fully accessible

The ivy-clad Pavillon de la Reine is one of the loveliest places to stay in Paris. Entering through the tranquil garden, it feels as if you are wandering into a rural idyll, far removed from the crowds on the Place des Vosges. The comfortable sitting rooms have gentle charcoal drawings of plants on the walls, enhancing the restful and unhurried atmosphere. There is also a beautifully designed Carita spa in the basement although the hotel mini-gym does play music. The massages and beauty treatments here tend to be quiet, however.

La Maison Montparnasse

53 rue de Gergovie, 75014 ☎ 01 45 42 11 39
www.lamaisonmontparnasse.com
Métro Pernéty **Bus** 58, 62
No disabled access, except for the garden

Despite the visually enervating bright pink, purple and orange colour scheme, this hotel is actually quite calm
and restful. The rooms are not huge but make up for this by having leafy views at the rear and there is a small garden
patio to enjoy an alfresco coffee and croissant with home-made jam for breakfast. Located near to Gare Montparnasse,
this hotel is a good place for a stopover en-route to warmer French destinations.

Rue du Temple Apartment

rue du Temple, 75004 ☎ 06 70 99 06 84
www.couette-et-cafe.fr **Métro** Rambuteau
Bus 29, 38, 47, 69, 70, 72, 74, 75, 76, 96
There is no wheelchair access to the apartment

Two enterprising French men own this nice apartment in
an historic building in one of the trendiest areas in Paris.
The comfortable bedroom is at the rear of the building so
is well away from any street noise. Rates are reasonable
and as this is a self-contained flat, you don't have to put
up with chattering guests over breakfast. There are some
great patisseries nearby, making this an inexpensive way
to enjoy being at home in the city.

Cité Véron Apartments

94 boulevard de Clichy, 75018
www.homelidays.com **Métro** Blanche, Pigalle,
Place de Clichy **Bus** 30, 54, 67, 74
No disabled access

It might seem strange to suggest a place to stay near
busy Place Blanche, but these two attractive apartments
are tucked down cité Véron, a peaceful cul-de-sac behind
the main boulevard. Although you can see the back of the
familiar red Moulin Rouge windmill sails from one of the
windows, these are both very quiet places to stay. The
studio overlooks a small, leafy garden and is furnished with
everything you would want from a bijoux Parisian apartment.

Rue Thorigny Apartment

rue Thorigny, 75003 ☎ 01 42 51 19 80
www.meetingthefrench.com
Métro Saint-Sébastien Froissart, Chemin Vert, Filles de Calvaire
Bus 20, 65, 96
Despite there being a lift inside the modern building, there is a small step to get into the complex

This modern apartment is ideally situated near to numerous galleries for contemporary art enthusiasts. Just round the corner from rue Saint Claude, this is a beautifully designed flat full of objets d'art and stylish curios. The owner is also very enthusiastic about introducing the local area to visitors, that is if you can bear to tear yourself away from the very attractive interior. On arrival you'll find a delicious breakfast from a local boulangerie waiting for you in the beautiful kitchen.

Rue Vaneau Apartment

rue Vaneau, 75007
www.sabbaticalhomes.com
Métro Sèvres-Babylone, Varenne and
Saint-François-Xavier **Bus** 69, 87
No disabled access

This exceptionally quiet apartment overlooks the rarely
used garden of the Hôtel Matignon, the official residence
of the French Prime Minister. Other than the occasional
garden party, the only sounds you will hear are birdsong
or the wind rustling the leaves in the mature chestnut
trees. The 19th-century apartment is close to the Rodin
Museum. It is also a very safe place to stay.

Rue Feutrier Apartments

rue Feutrier, 75018
Contact Alexandra Lord at saintsabin@gmail.com
www.sabbaticalhomes.com
Métro Château Rouge, Anvers, Abbesses **Bus** 56
The apartment is not accessible for wheelchair users

This studio apartment on the edge of Montmartre is an
exceptionally quiet place to stay. Close to Basilique
Sacré Coeur and to métro and bus routes into the centre,
there are numerous neighbourhood restaurants as well
as Square Louise Michel, a pretty city park, at the end of
the street. Another, slightly smaller, apartment is also
available to rent in the same street.

Hôtel du Jeu de Paume

54 rue Saint Louis en l'île, 75004 ☎ 01 43 26 14 18
www.jeudepaumehotel.com
Métro Pont Marie **Bus** 67, 86, 87
Excellent disabled access

Jeu de Paume translates as 'the game of real tennis', and
this lively pastime was played by King Louis IX in this very
building. Having fallen on hard times, the building was
restored a few years ago. Contemporary prints and small
bronze sculptures sit alongside fine antiques in the hotel's
visually stunning interior. There is also a small courtyard
to have breakfast outside on sunny days, making this feel
like a very special place to stay.

Hôtel de Sevres

22 rue de l'Abbe-Gregoire, 75006 ☎ 01 45 48 84 07
www.hoteldesevres.com **Métro** Vaneau, Saint-Placide,
Rennes, Sèvres-Babylone **Bus** 89, 94, 95, 96
There is a lift but no rooms especially adapted for
wheelchair users

This sophisticated hotel is just round the corner from
rue du Cherche Midi, a lively, interesting street with cafés
and shops selling unique, beautifully designed wares.
The rooms are immaculate and the staff friendly and
welcoming. There is a small spa in the basement where
you'll find one of the very few flotation cocoons in Paris
and, fortunately, this space is also open to non-residents.

Index of places by arrondissement